BODYBUILDING MEA

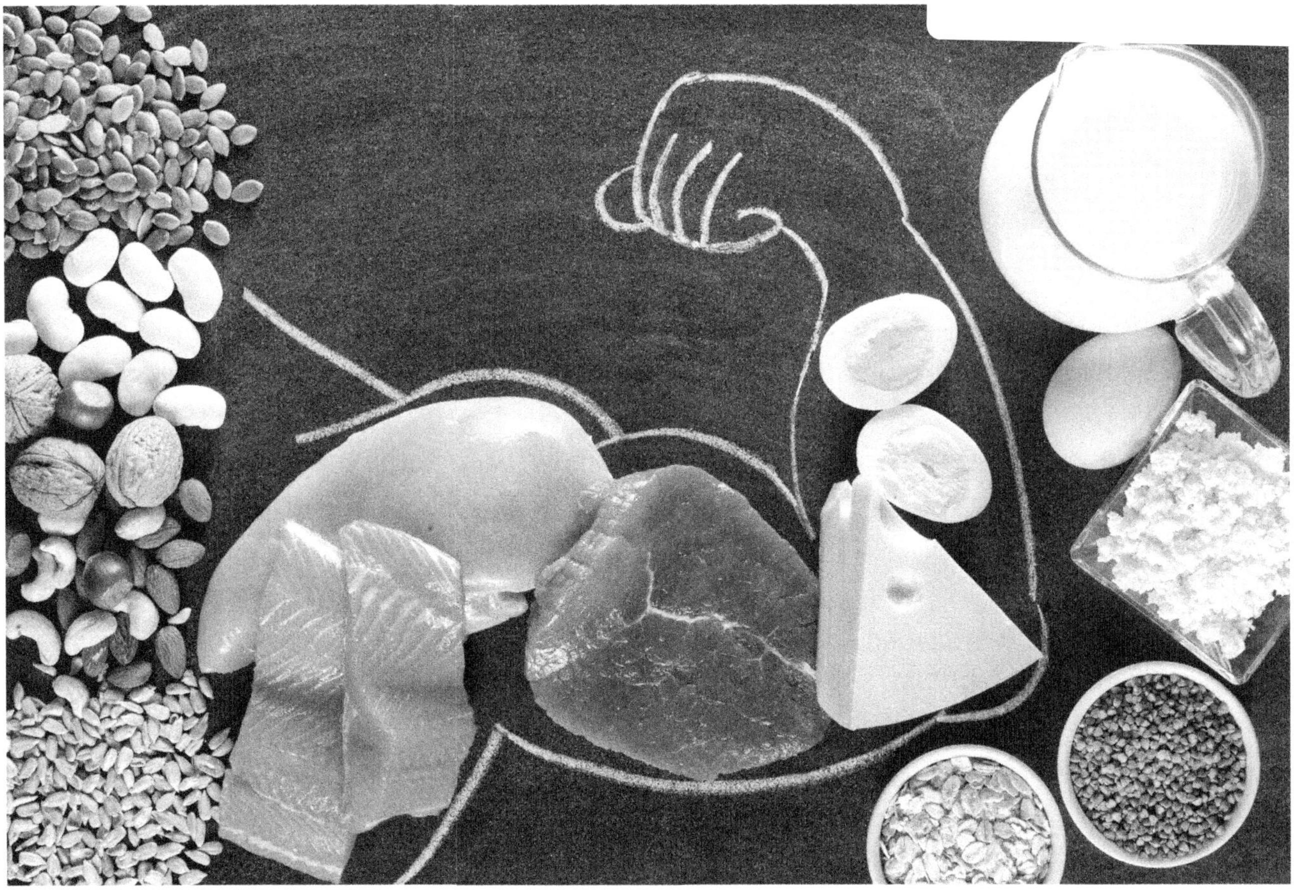

Fuel Your Muscle Growth with Protein-Rich Recipes: A Comprehensive Guide to Efficient Prep, Nutritional Mastery, and Varied, Tasty Fitness Feasts | Whit a 30-Day Meal Plan

MARK J. LEWIS

Table of Content

Chapter 2
The Food Preparation Command Center—Essential Tools 29

Chapter 3
The Magic of Meal Preparation—Time and Energy Efficiency 47

Chapter 4
Bodybuilding Recipes — Fitness Banquet

Chapter 5

Chapter 6

Chapter 7

Introduction
Succeeding With Meal Preparation

Welcome to our adventure of food and fitness. I'm Mark J. Lewis, a seasoned bodybuilder with a fierce love of physical training and a mastery of the culinary arts. I intend to impart to you a decade's worth of knowledge and expertise in the fields of food and fitness through the pages that follow.

For many people, preparing meals appears like a challenging process with several tiny details. It is the unidentified component that has propelled both my and many other bodybuilders' successes. Food is a science and an art that, when understood and applied, may drastically alter your results in the gym and your general well-being. It is not only a matter of feeding the stomach.

Because you understand how important it is to feed your body the correct meals, you have come to this page. Perhaps you have noticed a gap in your training program or you just want to boost your performance and general wellness. The solution to those questions may be found here. I'll lead you by the hand and demonstrate how, when, what, and why to eat. You'll learn the science and reasoning behind each nutritional option, how it affects your body and your bodybuilding objectives, and more, in addition to easy recipes.

You'll come to see the kitchen the way I do: as a place of limitless possibility where each ingredient, spice, and cooking method can support your bodybuilding endeavors. Here, the kitchen transforms into an area for experimentation, where each meal is a chance to advance toward your objectives.

Dive into each chapter with an open mind, ready to learn and be challenged by your existing eating and bodybuilding habits. It's more than just a cookbook; it's also a lifestyle guideline that will help you meet and, ideally, surpass your fitness objectives.

I want to be there for you at every turn, offering advice, tactics, and most importantly, the wisdom I've accumulated over the years. By the conclusion of this trip, I hope you will view meal preparation not as a duty but as a tool, a passion, and eventually an artistic endeavor that fuels your bodybuilding career.

So as you scroll through these pages, keep in mind that every word, every piece of advice, is designed with you and your success in mind. I am your guide, but you are the protagonist of this story. It is your passion, your dedication, and your effort that will lead you to success, and I am here to support you every step of the way.

You may wonder, what is the key to preparing meals in bodybuilding? Allow me to enter this exciting universe where each food, each ounce, has a purpose.

Bodybuilding is not just a passion, it's a lifestyle. And within that lifestyle, what we put in our mouths plays as fundamental a role as the time we spend in the gym. Yes, we can train at our highest intensity, putting in hours a week, but without proper nutrition, our efforts are diminished.

But why does meal preparation take such a central place? Simple: Preparation empowers us. It means power over our food, power over our choices, and finally power over our results.

Imagine this scenario: You finish an intense workout, your body is screaming for nutrients, and you find yourself with nothing prepared. It is easy to be tempted to go for the quickest, easiest, but not necessarily the most nutritious meal. Now, imagine that you come home and have a balanced meal waiting for you, designed specifically for your needs. The difference is remarkable.

This is just a matter of both convenience and accuracy. In bodybuilding, details matter. We talk about adjusting our diet to our needs, knowing exactly what and how much we are consuming. And this is where meal preparation becomes an invaluable tool.

Beyond precision, preparation gives us consistency. On the path to the body you want, consistency is key. It is not the sporadic efforts; it is the work day after day that makes the difference. By having your meals packed in advance, you can guarantee that your diet will remain consistent and in line with your objectives.

Making food for your family becomes a ritual in which you carefully decide what to feed your body. It is an act of commitment and self-care. It enables you to play with foods you might not have known but are crucial for bodybuilding, try new flavors and textures, and experiment in the kitchen.

You become aware that your connection with food alters as you go in this world. Though no longer required, it nonetheless forms a component of your education. Deep down, every meal is a chance for you to take care of yourself, advance toward your objectives, and demonstrate your dedication to this course of action.

An example of this dedication is meal preparation. A financial investment in oneself. And just as every exercise repeat counts in the gym, every meal you make with purpose puts you one step closer to the body and wellbeing you desire. It's a thrilling voyage, and I'm here to help you at every turn so you can make the most of each mouthful.

It is natural for you to wonder how this book while offering information, enhances your goals. I want you to understand that this book is not just a compendium of isolated recipes and tips, it is a comprehensive guide specifically designed to transform your body, your relationship with food, and your approach to bodybuilding.

As you navigate these pages, you'll find an in-depth exploration of the nutritional building blocks that underpin a bodybuilder's physique. The balance between proteins, carbohydrates, and fats is not something to be taken lightly. Each macronutrient plays an indispensable role in muscle development, recovery, and overall performance. But, beyond simply knowing them, you have to understand how to combine them on your plate, and how to make them work in synergy to maximize your results.

Water, that vital component, is not far behind in our exploration. Hydration is a powerful tool, and knowing its role in the muscle-building and recovery process is the key to taking your training to the next level. And yes, we'll be talking about the often-forgotten aspect of nutrition: caloric intake. Mastering this factor makes the difference between gaining lean muscle or simply gaining weight.

But we do not stay only in what is eaten. We delve into the how. The kitchen seems like a domain outside the gym, but I assure you that, with the right tools and a little ingenuity, it becomes your most powerful ally. You will learn to maximize your utensils, make your rice cooker an invaluable ally, and understand the guidelines for storing and preserving those dishes you prepare with so much love and dedication.

Efficiency has a prominent place in our journey. While it's true that bodybuilding takes time and effort, that doesn't mean we should spend endless hours in the kitchen.

Of course, what would a book on meal preparation be without recipes? But don't expect just a list. Each recipe you will find has been carefully selected and designed with the specific needs of a bodybuilder in mind. From energy-packed breakfasts to nutritious dinners, not forgetting those snacks that will help you manage hunger and pre- and post-workout meals that will be crucial in your daily routine.

If you've ever been curious about how bodybuilding champions prepare and what their relationship is to food, I'll give you unique insight. It is about my experiences and the secrets and strategies of those who have reached the pinnacle of this sport.

I am aware that there will be challenges, just as on any journey. You may probably encounter difficulties on your journey to flawless meal preparation because nothing is truly perfect. Here is a helpful approach to overcoming those obstacles, developing the habit of meal preparation, and maintaining consistency even in the face of hardship.

I will offer you a roadmap that works for those who are just starting, and for those who already have experience and are looking to take their passion to the next level. Whether you're looking to compete or just improve your physique, you'll find tips and strategies to further your journey.

All this and more await you in these pages. It is a trip that I have designed thinking about you, your goals, and your passion. It is a journey that I hope will inspire you, inform you, and most of all, empower you to achieve those bodybuilding dreams within you.

Chapter 1
Nutritional Principles for Bodybuilding

When I first started in bodybuilding, like many others, I enthusiastically dove into training routines, the mechanics of each lift, and the discipline that was required in the gym day in and day out. Over time, I realized an undeniable truth: The genuine art of bodybuilding goes beyond weights and machines. It is an art woven in the kitchen, in the choices we make in the supermarket, in the portions we serve on our plates, and, above all, in the knowledge we have about nutrition.

Nutrition is often the forgotten cornerstone of bodybuilding. As we obsess over numbers—the weight we lift, the reps we do, the days we train—we forget that what we eat is, in many ways, even more critical. Imagine for a moment that your body is like a high-end sports car. It doesn't matter how powerful the engine is or how aerodynamic the design is; if you put poor-quality fuel in it, it just won't perform at its best. The same goes for our bodies.

Every gram of protein, every carbohydrate molecule, and every drop of fat has a purpose. It's not just about "clean eating" or following the latest fad diet. It's all about understanding what your body needs, when it needs it, and how much. For over a decade, I have experienced on my skin, and with countless training partners, the difference proper nutrition makes to results. I can confidently say that a well-planned diet tailored to your goals accelerates your progress, improves your recovery, and ultimately defines the type of athlete you become.

In this chapter, we will delve into the fundamental pillars of nutrition for bodybuilding. I'll provide you with more specific, scientifically supported information about how each macronutrient affects our muscle growth in addition to basic guidance. We'll examine the interplay of protein, carbohydrates, and fat to show how they support and repair our muscles.

We'll talk about the value of being hydrated. In the beginning, I used to undervalue the significance of water. You'll discover that keeping a healthy amount of hydration is essential for effective exercise, quick recovery, and steady muscular growth.

We shall now explore the intricate realm of calories. This is a subject that often confuses me. Should you consume a surplus? How do you know if you are in a deficit? Which is the magic number? I'll guide you through these questions and more, helping you establish a solid understanding of caloric intake and its role in bodybuilding.

Throughout my journey, I have learned that bodybuilding is both a science and an art. It is the perfect union of physical and mental discipline. In many ways, nutrition is the bridge between these two worlds. As you open this chapter and embark on this journey with me, remember that every dietary choice you make is a piece of the intricate puzzle that is bodybuilding. I'm here to help you assemble those pieces as effectively and efficiently as possible.

Perfect Balance – Regulating Proteins, Carbohydrates, and Fats

Before explaining how to regulate proteins, carbohydrates, and fats, I want to present information that may be perceived as basic, but it is necessary because, precisely, it is essential for going to another level of knowledge.

Basics About Proteins, Carbohydrates, and Fats

In this segment, I'm going to walk you through everything related to protein, and then I'll move on to carbs and fat.

Proteins

Diving into the world of bodybuilding and fitness involves more than just lifting weights or doing cardio. It is a commitment to oneself, a promise to feed and nourish the body in the best possible way. In this journey of transformation, proteins emerge as one of the undisputed stars. But why is there so much talk about them? What makes them so necessary for those looking to shape their body and reach higher levels of performance? Let me be your guide on this in-depth journey of understanding protein and its cardinal role in bodybuilding.

The ABC of Proteins

Proteins are complex molecules, but before we delve into their many functions, we need to understand their basic structure. They are macromolecules made up of chains of smaller units called amino acids. Imagine a train made up of different wagons; each wagon would be an amino acid and the entire train, the protein. 20 different amino acids make up the proteins we eat and that our bodies use.

Of these, nine are "essential," meaning our bodies don't make it on their own and we must get it from food. These amino acids are necessary for many of our biological functions.

The Role of Proteins in Bodybuilding

Muscle repair and growth: Imagine that every time you train, especially when you do resistance exercises, you are creating small tears in your muscle fibers. These micro-lesions are, paradoxically, a good sign. They are evidence that you are pushing your limits and your body will respond by strengthening those fibers. And guess what helps in that repair and strengthening process? Proteins. They come to the rescue by providing the necessary amino acids to repair and increase the size of muscle fibers.

Biochemical functions: Proteins are related to muscles. They play roles in almost every process in our body. They act like enzymes, facilitating and accelerating chemical reactions; like hormones, sending messages and coordinating activities between different organs; and as carriers, transporting essential substances from one part of the body to another.

Defense and protection: Our immune system is highly dependent on protein. Antibodies, a special class of proteins, serve to identify and fight invaders such as bacteria and viruses. Without an adequate amount of protein, our ability to resist disease would be compromised.

Nutrient transport: There are specific proteins, such as the aforementioned hemoglobin, that have the crucial task of transporting oxygen from our lungs to all the cells of the body. But this is just one example. Many other proteins facilitate the transport of vitamins, minerals, and other nutrients, ensuring that every part of our body receives what it needs to function.

Quality and Origin of Proteins

Understanding that not all proteins are made equally is crucial. Even though we may obtain protein from both animal and plant sources, the amino acid composition varies. For instance, since they include all the amino acids in the right amounts, meat, fish, and eggs are complete protein sources. However, plant-based sources of protein like legumes and certain grains are deficient in one or more necessary amino acids. Vegetarians and vegans are not disadvantaged as a result of this. A comprehensive amino acid profile may be created by mixing several plant sources.

Why Is Protein Intake So Critical in Bodybuilding?

Bodybuilding is both an art and a science; it is not just about appearances. Every set, rep, and food is planned to bring out the best in the body. Proteins serve as the main building block for muscles in this plan.

Your body will require more protein as you advance in your bodybuilding adventure. Because protein promotes recuperation, cutting down on the amount of time between workouts and enabling you to exercise harder, you need more "building material" for those expanding muscles.

You'll discover that protein will be a constant along your path to a stronger and slimmer body—an ally you can always count on to help you achieve your objectives. It's a relationship that, properly nurtured, will only get stronger over time.

Carbohydrates

If protein is the cornerstone of muscle growth, then carbs are the fuel that keeps your engine running. In the context of bodybuilding and intensive training, understanding carbohydrates, and how to use them to your advantage, is essential.

Nature and Classification of Carbohydrates

Carbohydrates, often known simply as "carbs," are organic molecules made up of carbon, hydrogen, and oxygen. They are the main source of energy for many bodily functions and physical activities.

They are classified according to their structure and complexity:

Monosaccharides: These are the simplest carbohydrates. Glucose and fructose are examples. They are found in fruits and honey.

Disaccharides: Composed of two monosaccharide molecules. Sucrose (table sugar) is one example and is found in many processed foods.

Polysaccharides: These are complex carbohydrates. Cellulose, which forms the structure of plants, and starch, found in foods like potatoes and rice, are examples.

The Crucial Role of Carbohydrates in Bodybuilding

This is what you can get with a good carbohydrate intake:

Fast energy: During intense exercise, the body turns primarily to glucose for energy. Muscles store glucose in the form of glycogen, which is quickly broken down to meet the energy demands of a workout.

Recovery: After training, the glycogen stores in the muscles are depleted. Consuming carbohydrates after exercise helps replenish these stores, facilitating recovery and preparing the muscles for the next training session.

Refilling these reserves with carbs after exercise speeds up recovery and gets the muscles ready for the next training session.

Brain health: The brain uses glucose as its main source of energy. Adequate carbohydrate intake is required for cognitive function and mood.

Muscle preservation: When carbohydrate stores are low, the body begins to use protein for energy, which is not ideal for someone looking to build muscle mass. If you eat enough carbs, you can make sure that protein is used for building and repairing muscles, not for energy.

Carbohydrate Quality and Choice

Carbohydrates are not all made equal. While simple carbs, like table sugar, provide a rapid burst of energy, they also cause blood sugar levels to jump and fall. Contrarily, complex carbs produce a constant flow of energy since they are digested and absorbed more gradually. Foods high in complex carbs include oats, brown rice, and legumes.

Depending on the stage of training, a bodybuilder may choose to ingest a different type and/or quantity of carbohydrates. For instance, a larger carbohydrate intake might be chosen during a bulking phase, when the objective is to increase muscle growth. The amount of carbohydrates consumed may be decreased during a cutting phase, where the objective is to lose body fat.

In the end, carbs constitute an important dietary weapon for bodybuilders. They provide the energy required for rigorous exercise, aid in recuperation, and guarantee that the body performs at its peak. To get the most out of a tool, you must learn how to utilize it. As you continue on your bodybuilding journey, you will realize that having a balanced relationship with carbohydrates helps you achieve your goals and maintain optimal performance.

Fats

Over the years, fats have been demonized and misunderstood, especially in the realm of health and nutrition. Low-fat diets became popular, and many came to believe that consuming fat equaled weight gain. If there is something you should know, it is that fats are essential for the human body, especially for someone dedicated to bodybuilding. Fats generate energy and play crucial roles in hormone function, organ protection, and nutrient absorption.

Nature and Classification of Fats

Fats, technically known as lipids, are molecules composed mainly of carbon and hydrogen. They are classified according to the nature of their fatty acids:

Saturated fats: They are found primarily in foods of animal origin, such as meat and dairy products, and tropical oils, such as coconut oil. They are usually solid at room temperature.

Unsaturated fats: They are liquid at room temperature. They are divided into monounsaturated (found in oils such as olive) and polyunsaturated (present in fish, nut, and seed oils).

Trans fat: Mainly artificial and produced by a process that adds hydrogen to liquid oils to solidify them. They are found in many processed foods.

Cholesterol: A waxy substance found in the body and in some foods. Necessary for the formation of cells and hormones.

The Role of Fats in Bodybuilding

This is the role that fats play or should play in your diet:

Lasting energy: Although carbohydrates are the primary source of energy for the body, fats provide a denser source of energy, with 9 calories per gram compared to 4 calories per gram for carbohydrates and protein. Therefore, lipids are a great source of energy for strenuous, low-intensity activity.

Hormone health: The generation of hormones like testosterone, which is important for muscle growth and recuperation, depends on fats. Hormone levels for muscle building are optimized when healthy fats are consumed in suitable amounts.

Nutrient absorption: Fat is necessary for the body to absorb and use the fat-soluble vitamins A, D, E, and K. You might not receive the full advantages of these nutrients if your diet is deficient in fat.

Protection and isolation: Vital organs are protected by fats, which also assist in regulating body temperature and provide a reserve energy supply.

Choosing the Right Fats

It's important to realize that not all fats are created equal in terms of the health advantages they provide. The majority of your fat consumption should be made up of monounsaturated and polyunsaturated fats because they are typically the healthiest. These fats lower the chance of developing heart disease, raise cholesterol levels, and provide additional health advantages.

Saturated fat, on the other hand, should be consumed in moderation even if it shouldn't be totally avoided. Certain saturated fats, like those found in coconut oil, may be beneficial for your health, according to some studies.

Contrarily, trans fats must be kept to a minimum or removed entirely from the diet. They put people at higher risk for heart disease and other illnesses.

Fat shouldn't be viewed as an adversary in the context of bodybuilding, but rather as an ally. They offer a dense source of energy, support hormonal health, and ensure that your body can make the most of the vitamins and minerals you consume. As with any component of the diet, it is the quality and quantity that counts.

Why Should You Regulate Proteins, Carbohydrates, and Fats?

In the previous segments, it was already clear that proteins, carbohydrates, and fats, collectively known as macronutrients, are the dietary components that provide the energy necessary for the body to function. But why do you have to regulate and balance these macronutrients? Dive with me into this detailed exploration of the importance of maintaining proper balance:

Physical Performance Optimization

For someone involved in bodybuilding or any intense physical activity, macronutrient regulation maximizes performance. Proteins support muscle recovery, carbohydrates provide the energy needed for intense workouts, and fats ensure that long-term energy stores are available.

Metabolic Health

The proper balance between these macronutrients influences metabolic efficiency. For example, adequate protein intake increases thermogenesis (heat production) and resting energy expenditure, while carbohydrates influence blood glucose and insulin levels. Fats, especially essential fats, support cellular and hormonal health.

Weight Control

The composition and balance of macronutrients in the diet influence appetite, satiety, and ultimately weight control. For example, protein is often more filling than carbs or fat, which is useful for those looking to control their caloric intake.

Brain Function

Carbohydrates are the main source of energy for the brain. A constant and adequate intake of carbohydrates guarantees optimal brain function. Fats, particularly omega-3 fatty acids, are of great importance for brain health and cognitive function.

Disease Prevention

A balanced diet that regulates proteins, carbohydrates, and fats contributes to the prevention of various diseases, such as heart disease, type 2 diabetes, and certain types of cancer.

Dietary Flexibility and Adherence

By understanding the importance of each macronutrient and how to regulate it, you tailor your diet to your individual needs, preferences, and goals. This flexibility increases long-term adherence to healthy eating.

Challenges of Inadequate Regulation

Become aware of the importance or benefits of regulating proteins, carbohydrates, and fats:

Nutritional Deficiencies

While each macronutrient has a primary role, they are vehicles for many micronutrients. A low-fat diet results in deficiencies in fat-soluble vitamins such as A, D, E, and K. Limiting carbohydrates affects fiber intake, and not consuming adequate protein leads to amino acid deficiencies.

Metabolic Alterations

A diet consistently high in refined carbohydrates and sugars leads to insulin resistance. On the other hand, the lack of essential fats affects hormone production.

Long-Term Health Problems

A prolonged unbalanced intake increases the risk of chronic diseases. For example, diets high in trans and saturated fats are linked to heart disease.

Difficulties in Physical Performance

Without enough carbohydrates, the body feels fatigued during exercise. Inadequate protein intake slows down muscle recovery and affects muscle growth.

Ultimately, regulating and balancing protein, carbohydrate, and fat intake is not just a tactic for those looking to optimize muscle building or athletic performance. It is a fundamental strategy for anyone looking to live a healthy and enriched life. Understanding and respecting the integral role these macronutrients play in our health and well-being enables informed and effective dietary decisions.

Power Trio: Perfecting the Combination on Your Plate

As you have seen, these three macronutrients, when combined on the plate, act as a powerful trio, offering the individual benefits of each, and a synergy that enhances our well-being and performance.

Importance of Personalizing Your Dish Through a Good Combination

Although there is a general guide on how to balance these macronutrients, remember that each person has unique needs. Factors like activity level, health goals, and age influence how you should combine these energy sources in your diet.

Athletes and Bodybuilders

They require a higher amount of protein to support muscle growth and recovery, accompanied by carbohydrates to replenish glycogen stores and fuel your workouts. Fats will continue to be very important, especially to support hormonal health and provide long-term energy.

People With Weight Loss Goals

They could benefit from a diet moderate in carbohydrates, high in protein, and containing healthy fats. This combination improves satiety and reduces total caloric intake.

Individuals With Specific Medical Needs

People with diabetes, for example, need to pay special attention to their carbohydrate intake and balance it with protein and fat to maintain stable blood sugar levels.

The act of perfecting the combination of protein, carbs, and fat on your plate is an art, one that has the power to nourish the body, to transform your health and well-being.

Tips for Personalization and Combination of Proteins, Carbohydrates, and Fats

Each body is a different universe, with specific needs according to its daily activity, genetics, age, and health or performance goals. But regardless of those variables, many general rules of thumb and tips can help maximize the benefits of protein, carbs, and fat. Here are some guidelines and tricks for customizing and combining these macronutrients:

Clear Objectives, Clear Diet

To Increase Muscle Mass

Increase protein intake and be sure to combine it with carbohydrates, especially post-workout, to restore glycogen stores and facilitate protein synthesis.

To Reduce Body Fat

Consider a diet with moderate carbohydrates, high protein to preserve muscle mass, and healthy fats to maintain satiety.

To Maintain Weight

Find a balance between these three macronutrients that align with your daily activity level.

Combinations for Every Moment of the Day

Breakfast

Combine protein (eggs, yogurt) with complex carbohydrates (oatmeal, whole wheat bread) and healthy fats (avocado, nuts). This gives you sustained energy to start the day.

Pre-Workout

Prefer fast-absorbing carbohydrates and light proteins. A banana and whey protein shake is a great option.

Post-Workout

Prioritize protein and carbohydrates to restore energy stores and aid muscle recovery. Opt for chicken breast with sweet potato or quinoa, for example.

Dinners

Focus on protein and fat, reducing carbohydrate intake, especially if your activity will be limited before bed.

Listen to Your Body

Learn to interpret the signals that your body gives you. If you feel constant fatigue, you may be eating insufficient carbohydrates. If you stagnate in muscle growth, you may need more protein.

Prioritize Quality

Proteins

Opt for lean sources such as chicken, turkey, fish, legumes, and low-fat dairy. Consider high-quality protein supplements if necessary.

Carbohydrates

Prefer complex carbohydrates (oats, quinoa, legumes, and fruits) instead of simple ones (sugars, soft drinks).

Fats

Monounsaturated and polyunsaturated fats, present in olive oil, nuts, seeds, and fish, are your allies. Limit saturated fats and avoid trans.

Experiment and Adjust

Start with a basic macronutrient ratio, such as 40% carbs, 30% protein, and 30% fat. Over time, adjust according to your needs and goals. Nutrition tracking tools and apps are helpful for this.

Don't Fear Fats

For a long time, fats got a bad rap. But they are necessary for hormonal, brain, and cellular health. Just choose healthy sources and moderate the amounts.

Continuing Education

The science of nutrition is dynamic. Stay informed about the latest studies and findings to adapt and refine your diet according to new evidence.

In the end, the key is finding a balance that works for you and adapting it as your body and goals change over time. With dedication and focus, you'll master the art of combining and customizing these three macronutrients for optimal health and performance.

Hydration Takes Command: The Role of Hydration in Bodybuilding

Often underestimated, hydration is, in fact, a factor in performance, recovery, and muscle growth.

The human body is composed, on average, of 60% water. Every cell, tissue, and organ requires water to function. Muscles, specifically, are made up of approximately 75% water, which highlights the importance of hydration in muscle health.

These are the benefits of good hydration:

Muscle Function and Performance

Water facilitates electrical conduction in the body, which is crucial for muscle contraction. Dehydration, even mild, reduces muscle strength and endurance, limiting an athlete's ability to train intensely. Dehydration leads to muscle cramps, a hurdle for any bodybuilder.

Nutrient Transport

Blood, which is mostly water, carries oxygen and nutrients to muscle cells. Proper hydration ensures that blood can flow freely, delivering amino acids, glucose, and other nutrients to the muscles to fuel energy, recovery, and growth.

Thermoregulation

When lifting weights, the body produces heat. Sweat, a natural response to cooling the body, is made up primarily of water. If you're not hydrated, your ability to sweat, and therefore regulate your body temperature, is compromised. This leads to overheating, which is dangerous, and negatively affects your performance.

Joint Lubrication

Water plays a role in lubricating joints. Lifting weights puts stress on your joints, and proper hydration helps keep them lubricated, reducing the risk of injury and ensuring smooth movement.

Detox

The kidney, the main detoxification organ, relies on water to filter out toxins and metabolic waste, such as lactic acid produced during intense exercise. Adequate hydration facilitates this cleansing process, helping the body to recover faster and prepare for the next training session.

Cell Protection

Muscle cells, like all cells in the body, need a proper balance of fluids to function. Proper hydration ensures that cells can operate efficiently, supporting protein synthesis and other anabolic processes for muscle growth.

How to Stay Hydrated?

While hydration is very important, the exact amount of water a person needs depends on their weight, gender, activity level, and environmental conditions:

Listen to Your Body

Thirst is an obvious indicator, but don't expect to feel thirsty before you drink. Urine is a good indicator: If it's clear or pale yellow, you're generally well-hydrated. If it's dark, you probably need to drink more water.

Increase Intake on Training Days

During intense training days, your need for water increases. Drink before, during, and after the session.

Eat Foods Rich in Water

Fruits and vegetables like cantaloupe, cucumber, and spinach contribute to your daily fluid intake.

Keep a Balance on Electrolytes

Water is a timely necessity, as are electrolytes, especially when you sweat a lot. Consider sports drinks or electrolyte-enriched waters after particularly intense or long workouts.

Navigating Caloric Intake: A Route to Success

Calories, in particular, tend to be the main focus of many dietary discussions. How many calories are in this? How many calories did I burn during that workout? While the amount of calories is useful for understanding, another dimension, of the utmost importance, is often overlooked: caloric quality.

In its simplest form, caloric quality refers to the nutritional quality of the calories we consume. It is not just a matter of "how many" calories we are eating, but "where" those calories come from. Two foods could have the same caloric content but offer completely different nutritional value.

Consider two 200-calorie options: a chocolate bar and a quinoa dish with vegetables. If we only consider the calories, these two seem equivalent. When we analyze the caloric quality, we notice big differences. While chocolate might offer quick energy due to its sugars, quinoa with vegetables provides a wide variety of nutrients, including protein, fiber, vitamins, and minerals.

Foods of high caloric quality are usually rich in micronutrients. These are required for numerous biological functions, from energy production to protection against disease. Micronutrients, which include vitamins and minerals, are not measured in calories but are critical to our health.

On the other hand, there is nutritional density, which refers to the amount of nutrients provided by a food with its caloric content. Nutrient-dense foods offer more nutrients per calorie, which means you're getting more nutritional "punch" for every calorie consumed. For example, spinach, loaded with vitamins, minerals, and antioxidants, is nutrient-dense.

Although high-calorie foods are a bit more expensive up front, the investment is well worth it. You're not paying for better taste and freshness; you're paying for the long-term health benefits. When you reduce the risk of disease and improve overall well-being, you could find yourself saving on medical costs down the road.

To end this chapter, I want to leave you with a series of practical tips that will help you improve your caloric intake:

- Prioritize whole foods; these, in their most natural form, unprocessed or minimally processed, tend to have a higher nutritional density.
- Avoid added sugars; they provide "empty" calories with no nutritional benefit.
- Choose healthy fats, such as avocado, nuts, seeds, and olive oil instead of saturated and trans fats.
- Choose cooking methods that preserve or enhance nutritional value, such as steaming, sautéing, or roasting, rather than deep frying.
- Become familiar with reading labels to identify unwanted ingredients and make sure you're choosing products with the best nutritional value.
- Use herbs and spices to enhance the flavor of your meals. They add flavor without extra calories, and many herbs and spices have health benefits on their own.

Keep in mind that the diversity of foods guarantees a broader spectrum of nutrients. Try to eat different colors of fruits and vegetables, which indicate a variety of antioxidants and phytonutrients. In this sense, having a weekly meal plan helps you ensure that you are incorporating a variety of nutrient-dense foods and avoiding less healthy options for lack of preparation

Although it is more expensive, investing in organic products or buying directly from local producers improves the nutritional quality of your food, by offering you fresher products that are less exposed to pesticides and chemicals.

Nutrition is the foundation that fuels your passion and effort in bodybuilding. Throughout this chapter, I walked you through the basics of an effective diet: protein, carbohydrate, and fat, not forgetting the crucial importance of proper hydration and understanding caloric quality.

You learned that each macronutrient plays a crucial role in your health and building your physique. Proteins are the foundation of your muscles, carbohydrates are your primary source of energy, and fats are essential for many of your body's functions. But it's about consuming these macronutrients with an understanding of the intrinsic quality that each one brings to your diet.

Hydration contributes to the proper functioning of your body, optimizing your performance and ensuring that your muscles are in their best shape.

The concept of caloric quality shows you that not all calories are created equal. Now begin to focus your attention on true nutrition.

I hope this chapter gave you a solid foundation on which to build your nutritional journey in bodybuilding. Every meal you eat is an opportunity to nourish your body, strengthen your workouts, and get one step closer to your goals. As you move forward, I encourage you to be willing to put into practice each principle, advice, key, and all the information that I will be sharing with you.

Chapter 2
The Food Preparation Command Center – Essential Tools

When you open your kitchen door, what do you see? For some, it is simply a space where food is prepared quickly and occasionally. For you, as a passionate about bodybuilding and fitness, it must be something more: a command center. Here, every appliance, every tool, and every utensil has a specific purpose to help you achieve your nutrition and fitness goals.

If you've ever tried to build something without the proper tools, you know how frustrating it can be. Perhaps you have all the ingredients and the knowledge, but without the right tools, the process is inefficient and even counterproductive. Similarly, to maximize your bodybuilding nutritional goals, your kitchen must be stocked with the necessities.

Of course, I don't mean you need a professional chef's kitchen worth thousands of dollars. I'm talking about tools and gadgets that will simplify your life, make meal preparation more efficient, and help you preserve the quality and freshness of your food.

If you think of an athlete working out in the gym, you probably envision the weights, cardio machines, and other specific equipment that make their workout easier. In this chapter, I invite you to think about your kitchen in the same way. Imagine your refrigerator, your oven, your rice cooker, and other utensils as the "machines" that enhance your nutritional performance.

For example, a kitchen scale seems like a simple object, but for you, it is a must. It allows you to accurately measure your portions, ensuring that you are consuming the proper amount of each macronutrient. Or think about airtight containers, which keep your meals fresh, allowing you to transport them safely, so you always have a nutritious meal on hand, no matter where you are.

And while some might view a rice cooker as a luxury or single-food cooking appliance, for you, it's a versatile tool used to prepare multiple meals and save time. After learning how to get the most out of it, you'll wonder how you ever lived without it.

You also need to master some intangible "tools": knowledge about how to store food, how to reheat your meals without losing their nutritional properties, and how to choose the right containers for each type of food.

I should mention that while investing in certain quality tools at first glance seems like an expense, in the long run, it is an investment in your health, your time, and of course, your bodybuilding goals. The right tools make the difference between a mediocre meal and a perfectly prepared, delicious, and nutritious meal.

For your bodybuilding journey to be successful, you must view your kitchen as an ally. Every time you walk in, you should feel empowered, knowing that you have everything you need at your disposal to prepare meals that are delicious and get you closer to your goals.

Now let me guide you through this chapter, where we'll explore in detail those tools that will transform your kitchen into your personalized command center. Together, we will ensure that every corner of your kitchen breathes efficiency, quality, and passion for bodybuilding.

Kitchen Aids for Meal Preparation

It's no secret that meal preparation plays a critical role in bodybuilding nutrition. But beyond the ingredients you select, the quality and functionality of the tools you use in your kitchen are very important. These will determine how efficient and versatile they will be when preparing your meals, and the quality and flavor of your dishes. A well-equipped kitchen is like a well-structured gym: Each piece has its purpose and, when used in an ideal way, enhances your results. Before we dive into the list, remember that investing in good utensils is just as crucial as investing in good ingredients.

The Benefits of Having Good Tools for Food Preparation

You must become aware that the preparation of meals in this context is like alchemy, in which each ingredient and applied technique play a fundamental role. But the true art lies in what you prepare, and how you do it.

The tools you use in the kitchen are your faithful allies on this journey. Why? Here I detail the benefits of having them:

Efficiency and Time Saving

The modern pace of life, combined with the demands of bodybuilding, puts us all in a constant race against the clock. The right tools allow you to do more in less time and improve the quality of each meal prepared.

Imagine trying to cut vegetables with a dull knife; it takes more time, requires more effort, and the results are less than ideal. But a well-sharpened knife turns this task into a simple and efficient process. This efficiency gives you those valuable extra minutes to invest in training or rest.

Portion Consistency

When we talk about bodybuilding, we cannot underestimate the importance of precision. An ounce seems insignificant, but for days or weeks, those little inconsistencies add up.

Measurement tools take the guesswork out of you and give you confidence that you're getting exactly what your body needs. This consistency is required to monitor your progress, make adjustments to your diet, and achieve your bodybuilding goals.

Nutrient Optimization

The real value of food lies in its nutrients. We can consume large amounts of food, but if the nutrients are lost in the cooking process, we are wasting its potential.

Tools such as steamers allow food to be cooked in a way that retains a greater amount of vitamins and minerals. When you maximize the retention of these nutrients, you ensure that every bite counts, fueling your body with everything it needs to recover and grow after each workout.

Versatility in the Kitchen

Having a wide range of tools at your disposal is like having a complete gym at home. It gives you the freedom to experiment, vary your routines, and avoid monotony. The same is true in the kitchen.

With the right tools, you'll be able to regularly change your cooking techniques, try new recipes, and discover flavors you never imagined. This versatility keeps your passion for cooking alive and helps you stick to a bodybuilding diet without feeling like you're sacrificing the pleasure of a good meal.

Waste Minimization

We live in a time where food waste is a global problem. As a bodybuilder, every ingredient you buy is an investment in your health and well-being.

The peelers and graters allow each product to be used to the maximum, extracting all its nutritional value. When you minimize waste, you are being economically efficient, and respectful of the environment and the resources it provides.

Security Improvement

The kitchen is a dangerous place if not handled carefully. A dull knife or an unstable frying pan leads to accidents. Investing in tools is a matter of efficiency, as much as security.

High-quality tools are designed to minimize risk and ensure you can prepare your meals without worry. By becoming familiar with these tools and learning how to use them, you will become a more competent and confident cook.

Creative Stimulation

An equipped kitchen becomes a space for experimentation and creativity. The right tools act like brushes in the hands of a painter, allowing you to create culinary masterpieces.

This creative freedom serves to maintain enthusiasm and interest in your diet. Try new combinations, adapt recipes, and generally enjoy the creation process. This stimulation benefits your taste buds, mind, and spirit.

Food Preservation

Freshness is key when we talk about nutrition. Tools that help in conservation, such as airtight containers, ensure that your preparations keep their flavor and nutrients intact for longer.

This is particularly useful for those preparing meals for several days. By prolonging the life of your dishes, you save time and money, ensuring that every meal is just as good as the first time you prepared it.

Caloric Control Facilitation

In bodybuilding, every calorie counts. It's not just about counting them; you need to make sure they come from the right sources. With the right measuring tools, you can accurately serve portions, ensuring you stay within your daily caloric limits.

This precision helps with progress, as even small deviations over time have a significant impact on your results.

Promotion of Autonomy

Being autonomous in the kitchen means having full control over what you eat. You do not depend on restaurants or prepared meals that are not aligned with your goals. This autonomy is empowering, allowing you to be more adaptable and flexible in your diet, adjusting to life's changing circumstances.

Promotion of Healthy Habits

Owning a full arsenal of kitchen tools motivates you to cook at home more often. Home-cooked meals tend to be healthier, less processed, and more tailored to your specific needs than store-bought options.

These daily decisions to prepare your food promote healthy habits that extend beyond the kitchen, influencing your overall health, well-being, and, of course, your bodybuilding results.

Tools You Should Definitely Have in Your Kitchen

Here is an extended list of utensils and implements:

Digital Kitchen Scale

It allows you to accurately measure ingredients, which is crucial for calculating macronutrient intake and calibrating your portions.

Quality Knife Set

A good knife makes a big difference. Invest in a set that includes a chef's knife, a bread knife, a paring knife, and a serrated knife.

Cutting Board

Preferably made of wood or thick plastic, which guarantees durability and makes it easier to cut food.

Quality Pans and Pots

Select those made of ceramic, stainless steel, or cast iron. They are essential for cooking evenly.

Hermetic Containers

They are used to store and transport your prepared meals. Look for those that are microwave-safe and BPA-free.

Rice Cooker or Multicooker

These devices facilitate the preparation of carbohydrates such as rice and quinoa, among others, and usually have multiple functions.

Steamer

A great way to cook vegetables and protein without losing nutrients and without the need for additional oils.

High-Performance Blender

Ideal for protein smoothies, sauces, soups, and other shakes.

Food Processor

It facilitates the preparation of sauces, hummus, chopped fruit, vegetables, and ground nuts.

Aluminum Foil and Cling Film

To preserve the freshness of food and to cook certain dishes in the oven.

Silicone Molds

Ideal for preparing healthy snacks, such as protein bars or muffins.

Kettle or Teapot

For those infusions that help digestion or simply to enjoy a tea.

Grill

Perfect for cooking meat, fish, and vegetables with a smoky flavor and without the need to add additional fats.

Grater

Useful for grating vegetables, cheese, or even citrus.

Squeezer

Whether manual or electric, it is used to obtain fresh juice from citrus fruits.

Thermos or Reusable Bottles

Keep your smoothies cool or your infusions hot when you're on the go.

Kitchen Spatulas and Tongs

These tools will make it easier for you to handle food during cooking.

Filters or Strainers

Essential for washing and draining foods such as legumes and grains.

Gauge Set

Measuring cups and spoons will help you be precise with amounts.

Hand Mixer

Perfect for mixing sauces and dressings, or even for beating egg whites.

Set of Bowls of Different Sizes

To mix ingredients, marinate meats, or simply serve salads.

Roller

Whether it's for rolling out dough or crushing meat, it's a versatile tool in the kitchen.

Kitchen Timer

The precision in cooking times influences the texture and flavor of your meals.

Cooking Shears

They are ideal for cutting fresh herbs, meats, and other ingredients with ease.

Vegetable Peeler

It facilitates the process of peeling vegetables and fruits with precision.

Molcajete or Mortar

Ideal for grinding spices and making pastes or sauces.

Vegetable Cleaning Brush

It helps efficiently clean root vegetables such as potatoes or carrots.

Seasoning Containers

Keeping your spices and seasonings on hand promotes a smooth cooking process.

Steam Baskets

They are placed inside conventional pots and are useful for steaming without the need for a specialized steamer.

Kitchen Thermometer

It helps you ensure that meat and fish reach the right temperature, guaranteeing both its flavor and its safety.

With this list, you will equip yourself with the fundamental tools to master the art of meal preparation in the world of bodybuilding.

Maximizing Your Rice Cooker

One such tool, often underestimated but incredibly versatile, is the rice cooker. Beyond its primary function of cooking rice, this appliance is your best friend for preparing a variety of nutritious and delicious dishes.

Rice is a complex carbohydrate, a source of energy that, when consumed properly, helps you maintain energy during your workouts and aids in muscle recovery. But did you know that your rice cooker has the potential to do much more than just cook rice?

Although the primary function of a rice cooker is, as the name suggests, to cook rice, the variety of foods that can be prepared with it is surprising: from breakfast oatmeal, quinoa, and couscous, to soups and stews. Some people have even used it to make steamed cakes and breads.

Tips for Perfecting Rice

Keep the following tips in mind and you will enhance or maximize the use of your rice cooker:

Rice Type

There are different types of rice and each requires slightly different amounts of water. Familiarize yourself with the specific instructions for your rice cooker and adjust based on the type of rice you are using.

Washing

Always rinse the rice before cooking. This removes excess starch and prevents the rice from becoming sticky.

Water Amount

Follow the manufacturer's recommendations for the rice-water ratio.

What Other Foods to Cook With the Rice Cooker?

To maximize this appliance, it is convenient that you know that other foods can be cooked in it, these are:

Cereals

The rice cooker is excellent for cooking other grains such as quinoa, bulgur, and barley. This allows you to vary your carbohydrate sources and experiment with different textures and flavors.

Legumes

Lentils and other types of legumes cook to perfection in a rice cooker. They are an excellent source of protein and fiber.

Steamed Vegetables

Many rice cookers come with a steamer tray. Place vegetables on this tray while you cook the rice, maximizing efficiency and preparing a complete meal in one appliance.

Breakfasts

Have you imagined preparing your breakfast in a rice cooker? Make oats by simply adding oats and water or milk and letting the rice cooker do the rest.

Maintenance Tips for Your Rice Cooker to Work Perfectly

To ensure that your rice cooker lasts a long time and works perfectly, you must take care of it.

Cleaning

Be sure to clean the rice cooker after each use. Most rice cookers have nonstick cookware that pulls out, making it easy to clean.

Storage

Store the rice cooker in a dry place to prevent moisture buildup and prolong its life.

Proper Use

Although it's tempting to experiment, always follow the manufacturer's instructions to ensure you're using your rice cooker safely.

It's time to see your rice cooker with new eyes and make the most of all the opportunities it offers!

Food Preservation Rules: Home Food Storage Guidelines

The correct preservation of food is essential to maintain its nutritional qualities, ensure its safety, and prevent foodborne illnesses. Bodybuilders, especially, depend on a constant supply of high-quality food to nourish their bodies. Therefore, knowing how to store these foods is important.

First Things First: Understanding the Enemy in Microbial Growth

Food is the perfect breeding ground for bacteria, yeasts, and molds. These tiny organisms are everywhere, and while some are beneficial, others are harmful. You must understand that these microorganisms, especially bacteria, tend to multiply rapidly under the right conditions.

On the other hand, temperature, humidity, and pH are the most relevant variables for microbial growth. For example, bacteria grow most rapidly in temperatures between 41°F and 140°F (5°C and 60°C), a range known as the ⊠danger zone.⊠ That is why refrigeration and cooking are tools in the fight against bacterial growth.

In this sense, prevention is the key; by reducing the time that food spends in the "danger zone" and by storing it well, you significantly minimize the risk of foodborne illness.

Now, know the rules to preserve your food:

The Importance of the Cold Chain

The "cold chain" refers to the series of steps that ensure that food is kept at safe temperatures from production to consumption. Any interruption in this chain, whether in transport, in the store, or at home, compromises the safety of food.

- Refrigeration: Fresh foods, such as meat, fish, and dairy, require specific temperatures to preserve their freshness and prevent bacterial growth. Storage space must be considered, avoiding overloading the refrigerator, which could prevent poor air circulation.

- **Freezing:** This is a technique that completely stops bacterial growth but does not kill the bacteria. When defrosting, do it safely, either in the refrigerator, in the microwave, or in cold water, to prevent food from entering the "danger zone."

Cleaning and Hygiene

Before thinking about advanced preservation techniques, master the basics. Hands, utensils, and food contact surfaces could be vehicles for contamination if they are not kept clean.

- Avoiding cross-contamination: It is crucial to separate raw foods from cooked or ready-to-eat foods. Using different utensils and cutting boards for each type of food, and washing them well after each use, prevents the transfer of microorganisms.

- *Proper storage:* Use airtight containers to prevent liquids from raw foods, such as meat or fish, from leaking and contaminating other foods.

Dry Storage

Just as perishable foods require care, grains, legumes, spices, and other dry goods have storage requirements.

- Avoid moisture: Dry foods and grains absorb moisture, which leads to the proliferation of molds. Storage in airtight containers and cool, dry places is convenient.

- **Pest control:** Flour, rice, and other grains attract insects. Keep these foods in sealed containers and regularly check their condition to prevent infestations.

Labeling and Rotation

Keeping track of when a food item was purchased or stored helps with freshness management. Labeling food with dates allows you to follow an efficient rotation system, ensuring that the oldest items are eaten first.

FIFO System (First In, First Out): This system, widely used in the food industry, guarantees that the oldest food is used first, reducing waste and ensuring freshness.

Vacuum Packaging and Preserving

Vacuum packaging removes air, which slows down oxidation and prevents bacterial growth. It is especially useful for meat and fish.

Canning and preserving techniques involve the use of heat to kill bacteria and other pathogens, allowing food to be conserved for months or even years without refrigeration.

Based on the following rules, I will share preservation tips by type of food:

Vegetables and Fruits

Vegetables and fruits are components of a balanced diet, offering a wide range of nutrients and vitamins. Despite its freshness and naturalness, not all of them have the same conservation needs. For example, while some tomatoes benefit from ripening at room temperature, others, especially when already ripe, need to be moved to the refrigerator to prolong their freshness.

Be aware that some fruits, such as apples and bananas, emit ethylene, a gas that accelerates the ripening of other nearby vegetables and fruits. Therefore, separation is essential. This ethylene production is useful if we want to speed up the ripening process of certain fruits, but if not handled properly, it causes premature losses.

Vegetables and fruits have a high water content. Therefore, maintaining proper humidity is crucial. Leafy green vegetables, for example, need a humid environment, while other vegetables and fruits need less humid conditions. Bags with holes or specific drawers in refrigerators regulate this humidity.

Rotation and checking: As with other foods, fruits and vegetables should be rotated and checked regularly to ensure they are consumed at their best and avoid waste.

Meat and Fish

Among foods, meat and fish pose some of the greatest risks in terms of bacterial growth and spoilage. They are susceptible to bacteria such as Salmonella and E. coli, and their texture and moisture are ideal for microbial growth.

- Handling and packaging: Handle with gloves or with well-washed hands. Once the meat or fish has been purchased, packaging must be considered. Aluminum foil, for example, is great for fish, while meats need a more airtight wrap to protect against contamination and maintain freshness.

- **Marinades and preparation:** If you decide to marinate meat or fish before cooking, it is crucial to do it in the refrigerator and not at room temperature. Any sauce or marinade that has come in contact with raw meats should not be reused unless properly cooked.

- ***The cut challenge:*** Each type of meat or fish, and different cuts or pieces, have different storage requirements. For example, a fatty fish like salmon has a shorter shelf life than a lean white fish.

Dairy and Eggs

Dairy products are especially sensitive to time and temperature. Although it is essential to check expiration dates, you must trust your senses. A yogurt starts to smell or look different even before it reaches its expiration date.

- Proper storage: In the case of eggs, some regions refrigerate them, while others do not. The important point is to maintain consistency. When they have been refrigerated, they should stay cold. For other dairy, avoid the refrigerator door, as temperatures fluctuate there more than inside the appliance.

- ***Cheeses and molds:*** Although some cheeses are made with mold and it is safe to eat, mold that appears unintentionally on cheese is dangerous. It's important to know when to cut off the mold or when to discard the cheese entirely.

- ***Alternative milk:*** Non-dairy milk, such as almond or soy milk, has different storage requirements than cow's milk. Although they are generally less perishable, they should be consumed within a similar timeframe to traditional milk after opening.

Grains and Legumes

Although these foods seem less perishable, they still require care. Moisture is the enemy, as it causes grains and legumes to go bad or, worse yet, attract pests.

- Optimizing freshness: Storing them in airtight containers is a great way to extend their shelf life and maintain their quality. In some cases, refrigerating certain grains, such as whole wheat flour, helps maintain their freshness.

- ***Preparation and soaking:*** Legumes generally require soaking before cooking. You should change the water regularly and store it in the refrigerator if the soaking process is long.

While some grains cook quickly, others, like certain legumes, require longer cooking times. It is essential to know these times to guarantee the safety and quality of the cooked food.

Spices and Condiments

Spices and seasonings are the backbone of many dishes, offering nuances and layers of flavor that transform a simple meal into a culinary feast. From salt and pepper to the most exotic herbs, they are elements that enhance the cooking and eating experience.

- Proper storage: Many spices, especially ground ones, lose their potency and flavor over time. To preserve freshness and aroma, it is ideal to store them in a cool, dry place away from direct light. Airtight containers serve to prevent moisture and other contaminants from affecting the quality of the spices.

- **Rotation and renewal:** Although dry spices do not "go bad" like other foods, they do lose their potency. It is advisable to regularly check their freshness and aroma, and renew them from time to time. If you tend to buy in bulk, consider dividing up and storing the bulk in a cool, dark place, while keeping smaller portions on hand for daily use.

Fresh herbs and spices, like cilantro or rosemary, have different needs. It is best to treat them like fresh flowers: Cut the stems a little, place them in a glass of water, and cover the leaves with a plastic bag, refrigerating if necessary.

Drinks

From water to juice to milk and spirits, each type of liquid has its storage requirements. Beverages vary drastically in their needs and therefore you should know the best practices for each.

- Preserving freshness: Drinks, especially natural ones without preservatives, such as certain juices, deteriorate quickly. Refrigerate after opening and consume within a short period. On the other hand, some beverages, such as certain wines, benefit from long storage.

Once opened, carbonated drinks, such as soft drinks, lose their fizz quickly. While they are still safe to consume, the experience will not be the same. Using special lids or transferring to smaller bottles helps to preserve a little more of that characteristic bubble.

Heating Foods: Guidelines for Safe Reheating

If you've ever experienced that unpleasant feeling after eating a meal that may not have been reheated correctly, you'll understand the importance of this process.

Safe reheating ensures that food is palatable and safe to consume. It is a common misconception that when food has been cooked it is free of any potentially harmful contaminants. In reality, food becomes contaminated again after cooking, with certain bacteria surviving the initial cooking process. If food is stored incorrectly or for too long, harmful bacteria develop. Therefore, correctly reheating food generates benefits. For this, follow these recommendations:

Suitable Temperature

The correct reheating temperature helps the food to preserve its organoleptic properties, as well as being a safety measure. Insufficient heat will not guarantee that any bacteria or pathogens present are killed.

The internal temperature of food is a more reliable reference than the external one. This is because the outside quickly reaches high temperatures, while the center may not have gotten hot enough. A kitchen thermometer is an ideal partner in this process, offering an exact measurement and helping to avoid unnecessary risks.

It must be emphasized that the goal is to reheat, not cook again. While we want our food to reach a safe temperature, we don't want it to overcook, which could alter its flavor and texture.

Use the Right Equipment

Each food has its particularities, and not all reheating methods are equally effective. You must choose the right equipment for each type of food. This ensures that the food is heated evenly, and influences its final taste and texture.

While the microwave is a quick and convenient tool, it's not always the best option. For example, meat or fish lose their juiciness if they are not reheated correctly. The microwave may not heat evenly, leaving cold spots that are a risk.

On the other hand, the conventional oven, although it takes more time, usually offers a more uniform heating, especially for larger or dense dishes. It is ideal for those foods that we want to keep a crispy surface, such as pizza or certain types of fish.

Uniform Heating

Heating uniformity is crucial for two main reasons: food safety and food quality. Uneven heating results in areas that have not reached the proper temperature, potentially dangerous to health.

In the case of the microwave, given its tendency to heat unevenly, it is advisable to stop the process halfway, stir the food, and then continue. This simple action improves the uniformity of heating and, therefore, the safety and flavor of the food.

The use of lids or cling film helps maintain moisture and promote more even heating. Make sure these materials are microwave-safe to avoid accidents.

Do Not Reheat More Than Once

The recommendation not to reheat food more than once is well-founded. Every time food is reheated, it is subjected to temperature fluctuations that are conducive to bacterial growth.

From a culinary point of view, each successive reheating tends to degrade the quality of the food, textures become mushy, and flavors begin to fade or change. Especially with protein-rich foods, the risk of overcooking and drying out is high.

Therefore, it is advisable to only remove from the refrigerator and reheat the portion that is going to be consumed. If it is known in advance that not everything will be consumed, it is better to divide it from the beginning and heat only what is necessary.

Pay Attention to Time

Time is a factor of great importance when it comes to reheating food. Too long causes food to become dehydrated or even burnt. On the other hand, not giving enough time does not reach the proper temperature, especially in the center of denser foods.

It is more reliable and safer to start reheating for a shorter time and then add time as needed. This allows more control over the process and reduces the risk of overheating.

Remember that not all foods require the same amount of time. While a pasta dish might only need a few minutes, a thick cut of meat or a denser casserole might take longer to heat through.

Consider the Humidity

Moisture is an important component of many foods. Food that was originally moist or juicy may become dry or rubbery if reheated without regard to moisture.

An effective technique when using the microwave is to add a cup of water to the appliance while it is reheating. This helps maintain a humid environment inside the microwave, which prevents food from drying out.

For those foods that benefit from a little extra moisture, like rice or certain types of fish, adding a little splash of water or broth before reheating does wonders in terms of texture and flavor.

The remaining points would be addressed similarly, following the format of three paragraphs per point, going deeper into each topic to offer a complete understanding.

Avoid Overheating

While it seems like an easy solution to heat your food to a very high temperature to ensure it's hot on the inside, this could backfire. Overheating changes the texture of food, making it dry or rubbery, causing loss of nutrients.

A balance must be found between making sure food is hot enough to be safe and not getting it so hot that it loses its flavor and nutritional quality. In general, it's best to go for gradual, controlled heating, checking the internal temperature with a kitchen thermometer if possible.

Although the technology of modern household appliances allows us to heat quickly, one must be cautious. Using the oven, stove, or microwave at full power is not always the best option. Sometimes slow, steady heating produces better results.

Sauces and Liquids

Sauces and liquids are a challenge when it comes to reheating. On the one hand, they must be very hot to guarantee safety, but they must not boil too much and alter their flavor or consistency.

A good technique for reheating sauces is to do it over low heat in a saucepan, stirring frequently to ensure even heating. This ensures that it heats up as it should and helps preserve the original texture and flavor of the sauce.

In the case of soups or broths, make sure that they are heated to a temperature that guarantees the elimination of possible bacteria. But, again, you have to avoid simmering them for a long time, as this affects their flavor and texture.

Fried or Crunchy Foods

Reheating foods that were originally fried or have a crispy texture is very difficult. Microwaving, while fast, tends to make these foods mushy, losing their crunchiness.

An excellent option to reheat this type of food is to use a conventional oven or a toaster. The dry heat provided by these appliances maintains or even restores that much-desired crunchy texture.

You have to be careful with time and temperature. Although we want the food to recover its crunchy texture, we do not want it to dry out or burn. Constant checking and perhaps turning halfway through cooking ensures optimal results.

Caution With High-Risk Foods

Some foods are at higher risk of harboring bacteria than others, such as red meat, poultry, and eggs. With these foods, you want to make sure they reheat well and reach a safe internal temperature.

It is not enough that these foods are hot to the touch on their surface. The internal temperature is what counts. A kitchen thermometer is an indispensable tool to verify it.

You must consider how long these foods have been stored and if they have been handled in the ideal way before reheating. Even if they reheat well, if they've been stored or handled improperly, they're still a risk.

With these additional points and the dive into each one, we should be closer to fully covering the guidelines for safe reheating in detail.

The Container Dilemma: Choosing the Ideal Container for Your Meals

Although selecting the appropriate container may seem easy, there are certain crucial factors to take into account to ensure the ease, freshness, and quality of your food.

Choosing the appropriate container may be a life-changing discovery for many people. Even while it can seem over the top to give such a high priority to something so unremarkable, consider this: Your containers are the guardians of your nourishment. They serve as a shield between the carefully prepared food and the outside environment, safeguarding it from contamination, maintaining its freshness, and ensuring that it is at its finest when it is time to consume.

Container Material

Choosing the material is the first step in selecting the ideal container. Plastic containers are common because of their portability and lightness, but it's important to choose those that are BPA-free because this chemical has been linked to a number of health issues. It is important to make sure they can be used in dishwashers and microwaves.

Glass containers, on the other hand, are a strong and healthful substitute. They are good at keeping food's flavor fresh and are stain- and odor-resistant. Glass is easily recycled and has good environmental qualities. However, others may find that its heavier weight and potential for breaking are drawbacks.

Size and Shape

Your food requirements and daily schedule will have a significant impact on the size and form of the container you select. You could want a container with divisions if, for instance, you frequently consume meals that have several ingredients, such as chicken, rice, and veggies. These help keep food fresh, separating various types of food, and preventing tastes from blending.

Size is crucial if you are controlling portions. Having different-sized containers will allow you to accommodate larger or smaller meals as needed.

Hermetic Closure

An airtight seal maintains the freshness of your food. A good container should close securely, preventing spillage and ensuring that no air enters, which could degrade the quality of the food. This feature is especially important for those who take their meals to work, the gym, or on trips.

Thermal Adaptability

If you frequently reheat your meals, have containers that can withstand sudden temperature changes. Some containers go directly from the freezer to the microwave, making it easy to prepare and eat your meals.

Durability and Useful Life

Investing in high-quality containers is expensive at first, but considering their durability and lifespan, the cost is justified. A good container will last for years if cared for, while a cheaper one could warp, discolor, or break in a much shorter time.

Aesthetics and Design

Although it may seem like a minor aspect, the aesthetics and design of the container influence your eating experience. An attractive, well-designed container makes it easy to organize and transport your meals and makes the dining experience more enjoyable. Think of it as a presentation of your food: A well-presented dish is always more appetizing.

Choosing the perfect container for your meals benefits you on your path to bodybuilding success. A suitable container will protect your investment of time and effort in the kitchen, will ensure that your food maintains its freshness and quality, and will make it easier for you to follow your nutritional plan wherever you are. The next time you prepare your meals, don't underestimate the power of a good container. It is more than just a kitchen utensil: It is your companion on this journey toward the best version of yourself.

Cooler Bags: Your Secret Ally for the Freshness of Food

Meal preparation is a meticulous choreography that takes time and effort, but there's one point you shouldn't neglect after cooking: ensuring your meals stay in perfect condition. Cooler bags stand as silent guardians, protecting the integrity of each dish you've so carefully prepared. As you immerse yourself in the world of bodybuilding, you'll soon discover that these allies are more than just bags.

At a basic level, these utensils have compartments that allow you to accommodate your meals. They are often accompanied by reusable ice or gel packs that work to maintain a low internal temperature. They are made of materials that insulate and protect their content from the outside world.

Their primary function is to keep food at a safe temperature, preventing it from entering a "danger zone" where pathogens thrive.

They come in a variety of sizes and configurations, from those ideal for quick snacks to those designed to store all-day meals. Robust materials, reinforced seams, and specialized storage areas ensure that your investment has a long useful life, accompanying you on your daily journey without wearing out easily.

Choosing to carry your food in refrigerated bags is an economic and ecological decision. On the one hand, you save the expense of buying food on the street, which is usually more expensive and less healthy. On the other, you help reduce waste by making sure your home-cooked meals are consumed at their optimum.

While function is key, aesthetics is not far behind. In today's market, the variety of designs and colors available is staggering. Choose bags that serve their purpose, and reflect your personality and style.

Having the right tool is just the beginning. It is crucial to know how to use it correctly. Make sure the ice or gel packs are completely frozen before putting them in the bag. Food should be stored in airtight containers to maintain freshness and prevent spillage. Cleaning the bag regularly maintains a hygienic and odor-free environment.

After this tour, I hope you have understood the relevance of each detail in managing your diet. It's not about what you eat, it's about how you do it. Organization, preservation and, above all, commitment to quality are pillars for those who seek excellence in bodybuilding.

The equipment in your kitchen and your preparation strategies are not only complements, they are extensions of your determination and a reflection of your seriousness toward your goals. Just like in the gym, where your choice of weights, routines, and techniques reflect your approach to muscle building, in the kitchen, every tool and method you adopt determines how you feed and nourish those muscles.

Likewise, always remember that, as a bodybuilder, you must understand that every gram of protein, every calorie, and every drop of water has a purpose.

As I close this chapter, I invite you to reflect on your current habits and consider how you could improve and optimize your food preparation. Remember, in bodybuilding, the kitchen is just as essential as the gym, and having the right equipment and knowing how to use it is the key to unlocking higher levels of success and wellness. Go with confidence, equip your kitchen, and take one more step toward your goals.

Chapter 3
The Magic of Meal Preparation—Time and Energy Efficiency

Entering the world of bodybuilding entails a series of changes, adaptations, and learning that go beyond the gym and exercise routines. One of the most transformative areas is, without a doubt, nutrition and how we manage our daily diet. In this chapter, we dive into a facet of the nutrition journey that often takes a backseat: meal preparation. And while it doesn't always get the limelight it deserves, its impact on our time and energy efficiency is unparalleled.

When we talk about meal prep, we mean the strategy of planning and cooking meals in advance, usually for a week or at least several days. Imagine always having your dishes ready, without having to spend hours in the kitchen every day, avoiding impulsive decisions that could divert you from your nutritional goals.

For those who lead busy lives, and for those who are serious about bodybuilding, this strategy becomes an invaluable ally. Imagine the peace of mind of knowing that after an intense workout, your food is already ready, just waiting to be served or reheated. No more guessing what to cook or hasty decisions that could lead you to choose less nutritious options.

Planning our meals has transformative power. It becomes an act of self-care, where you make sure that no matter how busy your day is or how intense your training has been, you will always have a meal that is balanced and aligned with your goals. The time spent one day a week on this activity saves hours on the following days and reduces the stress of having to cook under pressure.

We have complete control over what we eat when we plan our meals. We are free to customize each ingredient, each serving size, and each cooking technique to suit our requirements and preferences. Because of this independence, we can make sure we are eating just the foods that will help our bodies heal, develop, and flourish.

There are yet more advantages. Meal preparation lessens the need for daily cooking and frees up our energy for other pursuits, such as exercise, rest, or just taking time to unwind. It is a device that enables us to replenish our energy.

The economy is another perk. You may take advantage of bargains, decrease food waste, and save money by purchasing and preparing in quantity. When you are certain of what you need, making purchases becomes more strategic and you stop making impulsive or wasteful purchases.

As we progress through this chapter, I'll guide you through the art of meal prep, showing you how it's a powerful tool in your bodybuilding arsenal. With practical tips, tricks, and techniques, you will discover how to transform this activity into one of your best allies to achieve your goals. On this journey, every detail counts, and having your nutrition under control is one more step towards your success in bodybuilding.

Supermarket Adventures: Strategies for a Successful Shopping Experience

The act of grocery shopping involves considerably more than just selecting items from the shelf and adding them to a cart. It is the first step in the process of preparing your supper. Your dietary plan will be directly impacted by the choices you make here. Here are 7 step-by-step tactics that will alter your viewpoint on this regular activity to help you make the most of your time and guarantee the effectiveness of your purchases.

Plan Your Visit

You must be certain of your needs before starting your excursion to the grocery store. Home is where this process starts. Examine your refrigerator and pantry, and think about the meals you want to make in the upcoming days. You can see the materials you already have and those you need to acquire thanks to this degree of organization.

A thorough shopping list, on the other hand, serves as a lighthouse in the dark store. Your list becomes a tool to help you stay on course when there are so many possibilities, detours, and temptations around. You may make a clear plan for your shopping experience by writing down everything you need. A well-planned list reveals mental discipline and distinct nutritional objectives. With it, you stay on track by avoiding detours and impulsive purchases.

Utilize tools that assist you in tracking, organizing, and even receiving recommendations based on your dietary choices and nutritional objectives. These digital tools provide a degree of versatility that is difficult to match with conventional techniques, making them perfect for mobile users.

Know the Aisles

Although they are similar in many respects, each supermarket has its own layout and structure. Although you would assume that all supermarkets are alike, there are really small variations in the way items are displayed, where specific areas are located, and how the aisles are laid out. To maximize efficiency, it helps to become familiar with the store you frequent. Look at the layout of the aisles, where certain products are located, and what is the most efficient route to get everything you need.

A common feature in many supermarkets is that fresh foods, such as fruits, vegetables, meat, and fish, are often located on the perimeter of the store. Starting your tour through these areas ensures that the healthiest and freshest foods are added to your cart first. The more time you spend in these sections, you establish a solid foundation for your diet and expose yourself less to processed products that tend to be found in the center aisles.

We all have our weaknesses, and supermarkets know it. For this reason, they place certain products, such as chocolates, candies, or snacks in strategic places, such as at the end of the aisles or near the cash registers. These are high-temptation areas. By being aware of these areas and recognizing your weaknesses, you make informed decisions about how much time to spend near them or even avoid them altogether. Self-awareness is the key to staying firm in your decisions and not falling into unnecessary temptations.

With proper planning and detailed knowledge of the terrain, your trips to the grocery store become less of a chore and more of a well-orchestrated experience that supports your nutritional goals. Preparation and familiarity are the keys to making shopping a productive and enjoyable activity.

Buy During Low Influence Hours

The rhythm of a supermarket varies depending on the time of day, on some occasions, the aisles are full of carts and people in a hurry. At other times, tranquility reigns. Choosing to do your shopping during these off-peak hours gives you numerous benefits, from more room to move to fewer distractions that can lead you to stray from your list.

At off-peak hours, you're free to peruse each shelf. Without crowds, reading nutrition labels becomes easy and pressure-free, allowing you to make informed decisions.

Fewer people means less waiting. Checkout lines are shorter, and the overall checkout process becomes much faster. Thus, what could have been an hour-long task is significantly reduced, freeing up time for other important activities for you.

Meet and Take Advantage of Promotions

Finances are an important factor in the bodybuilding journey. With the constant need for high-quality food, it's smart to take advantage of any opportunity to save. Supermarkets usually launch promotions, discounts, and special offers that are very beneficial for your pocket.

Many establishments offer loyalty programs that reward regular customers with exclusive discounts, coupons, or points that are redeemed. Enrolling in these programs puts you in a privileged position to learn about these offers firsthand.

If a product you consume frequently is on sale, it is a good idea to purchase more than one unit. This practice, if done wisely, ensures that you always have your favorite foods on hand and make the most of the deals. Of course, you must ensure that the products do not expire before consuming them.

Efficient purchases are those that are well-planned. Knowing when to go and how to take advantage of promotions puts you several steps ahead in your mission of maintaining a proper bodybuilding diet.

Focus on Seasonal and Local Products

Seasonal and local products arrive at the supermarket at their peak of freshness and flavor. They have been harvested at the right time, so they offer a higher concentration of nutrients. For someone committed to bodybuilding, consuming nutrient-dense foods is a crucial aspect of their diet.

Keep in mind that opting for local food means supporting the farmers and producers in your community. You contribute to the economic development of your region and become part of a sustainable cycle, where production and consumption support each other.

Imported or out-of-season foods often travel long distances before reaching supermarket shelves. This implies a high consumption of fuel and a greater emission of greenhouse gases. Choosing seasonal and local products minimizes this impact, encouraging a more conscious consumption, and respect for the environment.

By focusing on what's available in each season, you broaden your culinary horizons. Each season brings with it a new range of products to experiment with, allowing you to vary your diet and discover new dishes that align with your bodybuilding goals.

Analyze Labels

Although nutrition labels seem like a puzzle at first, learning to interpret them gives you the power to select foods that align perfectly with your nutritional goals. It is not enough for a product to be advertised as "healthy." It is necessary to go further and understand exactly what you are incorporating into your body.

Always remember that labels provide detailed information about the amount of protein, fat, and carbohydrate in a product. But that's not all: they show the presence of vitamins, minerals, and other compounds that are crucial for the optimal functioning of the body. Having this information at your fingertips allows you to make informed decisions about your diet.

In the search for quality food, you must keep an eye out for undesirable ingredients. Many processed products contain additives, preservatives, and other compounds that are not beneficial to the body. By reading labels, you identify and avoid these ingredients, opting for purer, healthier alternatives.

Sometimes you may find yourself in a situation where you have to choose between two similar products. Analyzing their labels allows you to compare them at a nutritional level and choose the one that best suits your needs. Over time, this ability becomes second nature and makes shopping a much more seamless and efficient experience.

Mental Preparation: The Right Attitude When Shopping

Going to the supermarket with a clear and focused mindset is more than just a tactic, it's a way of life. Each product you select has a direct impact on your well-being and fitness goals. When you are aware of this, every visit to the supermarket becomes an extension of your training and your commitment to bodybuilding.

From now on imagine how each food will benefit you, how it will translate into energy, how it will help muscle recovery, or how it will influence the construction of lean mass. This visualization, more than any list, will guide you to the right choices.

Keep in mind that in a supermarket, temptations are in every aisle. Offers, flashy products, or those that appeal to nostalgia or momentary cravings can divert you from your path. Maintaining a steady, focused attitude helps you navigate these challenges and stay true to your nutritional plan. In this sense, remembering why you are doing what you are doing is a powerful tool. Every time you choose a healthy food over a less beneficial one, you are reaffirming your commitment to your health, your body, and your long-term goals.

In the same way that you face a workout with determination and focus, face your shopping experience. Consider each food choice as a repetition, each correct decision as a completed series. This mindset will transform your shopping experience from being a mundane chore to an integrated part of your training. Appreciating the abundance and variety of food available is one way to nourish your mind while nourishing your body. Being grateful for the opportunity to make healthy food choices, for having access to nutritional information, and for being able to make informed decisions creates a positive attitude that extends beyond the supermarket.

On the other hand, being inquisitive about food, its origins, its benefits, and its uses makes you a more informed shopper. Investigate, ask questions, and constantly learn. This curiosity leads you to discover new foods, new recipes, and ways to optimize your diet for bodybuilding.

Lastly, to build the right mindset, just as bodybuilding requires patience to see results, the shopping experience requires it; instead of rushing through the aisles, take the time to read, choose, and decide. This patience will be reflected in the quality of the food that ends up in your cart.

Menu Planning: Success Plan

Menu planning represents a pillar in the life of any bodybuilder who seeks to optimize their diet. A well-worked and toned body is the result of both hours in the gym and proper nutrition. Aligning diet with specific training needs is an art that requires attention and dedication.

Imagine knowing that after an intense workout, the food you eat is exactly what your body needs to recover and grow. This is what menu planning offers bodybuilders: a practical guide of what to eat, when to eat it, and in what quantity. Uncertainty is eliminated, nutrition is maximized, and you take a step toward that desired physical goal.

Although it may seem like a complicated task, it is an investment. With proper organization, the time spent planning meals saves countless hours throughout the week. No more impromptu visits to the store, no more meals that don't align with your nutritional goals. Remember that every bite you take is building the body you work so hard to achieve. Keep these recommendations in mind:

Assess Your Nutritional Needs

Nutrition is a wide field, and each person navigates it with different needs. Before venturing into menu creation, you must do some deep introspection and know your nutritional needs. Understanding what your body requires gives you the foundation on which you will build your plan.

First, you must determine your daily caloric expenditure. It is made up of your basal metabolic rate—the calories your body burns at rest—plus the calories burned during physical activity. Using online calculators or nutrition tracking apps, get an estimate of your daily calorie needs. From there, you can calculate how much you need to eat to maintain, gain, or lose weight, depending on your goals.

Your calorie intake is built on macronutrients. These are divided into proteins, carbohydrates, and fats. Each one plays a role in your diet and is essential for different functions of the body. For example, protein is crucial for muscle repair, while carbohydrates offer quick energy. Determining the proper ratio of these macronutrients is key. On the other hand, micronutrients, such as vitamins and minerals, support a variety of bodily functions, from immune support to energy production.

After determining your needs, reflect on your tastes and any dietary restrictions you have, whether due to allergies, intolerances, or ethical choices. A successful menu is one that you enjoy and stick with for the long haul.

Set Your Goals Clear

Knowing your nutritional needs is only part of the puzzle. The next step is to set clear and defined goals. The purpose of your eating plan becomes the beacon that guides your daily decisions, and without clear direction, it's easy to get sidetracked.

Ask yourself: What do I want to achieve with my diet? It could be something as simple as feeling better every day or as specific as preparing for a competition in a couple of months. Whatever your goal, write it down. Having it in writing gives you a visual and tangible reminder of why you are doing what you are doing.

As you move toward your goals, you may encounter roadblocks or discover new things about yourself and your preferences. Perhaps a particular type of diet doesn't suit you, or you discover a new food that you love. It is important to regularly reassess your goals and make any necessary adjustments. Adaptability is the key to staying engaged and motivated on the path to your goals.

There will be days when motivation will falter, or you will face temptations. Remembering why you set those goals in the first place will help you stay on track. Persistence is what separates those who achieve their goals from those who fall short.

A clear understanding of your nutritional needs and set goals puts you in a strong position to start planning your menu. These two pillars offer you the foundation on which to build a diet that will nourish you and help you flourish.

Organization and Structure of the Menu

Creating a menu requires a structured approach. It's like building a house; you need a blueprint before you start building. Organizing your menu systematically will help ensure that all of your nutritional needs are met and that you stay within the guidelines you have set for yourself.

Divide your menu into breakfast, lunch, supper, and snacks as a good place to start. By doing this, you may concentrate on each meal separately and make sure that it fulfills a certain amount of your daily requirements. For instance, if you want energy right away in the morning, you can eat more carbohydrates for breakfast and more protein for dinner to support muscle repair over the night.

You should switch up the items you use to preserve nutritional balance and prevent boredom. Over the week, introduce various types of protein, carbs, and fats. This guarantees a wider range of nutrients and enables a deeper and more diverse culinary experience, adding excitement to your meal plan.

Consider the preparation when you have a clear notion of the meals and ingredients you want to use. Some ingredients may require soaking, marinating, or otherwise preparing before cooking. Anticipating these steps will save you time and stress when cooking.

Consider the seasonality of the food, so you will have fresher and cheaper products, and you will vary your menu according to the month or season of the year. Rotation is an effective way to ensure you get a variety of nutrients and not get stuck in a monotonous eating routine.

Balance Between Flavor and Nutrition

Nutrition is a critical part of menu planning, but taste plays a big role. After all, if you don't enjoy what you're eating, you're more likely to deviate from your plan. Finding a balance between flavor and nutrition is therefore central to the success of your meal plan.

Processed foods, while convenient, often contain additives, preservatives, and other unwanted ingredients. Cooking from scratch gives you full control over what you're putting into your body, allowing you to adjust dishes based on your preferences and nutritional needs, ensuring you get the best of both worlds: flavor and nutrition.

The method you choose to cook your food influences its flavor and nutritional value. Roasting, boiling, steaming, sautéing, or slow cooking are just a few of the many methods available. Each imparts a distinct flavor and texture to food. Experiment with different techniques to find the ones that best bring out the flavor of your ingredients without compromising their nutritional value.

Even with the best planning, you may find that some dishes are not to your liking or that certain food combinations do not suit you. You must be receptive to these signals and be willing to make adjustments as necessary. Refining your menu over time, taking into account both taste and nutrition, will lead you to a meal plan that you'll truly enjoy and stick with for the long haul.

With meticulous organization and a balance between flavor and health, your menu won't just be a set of randomly chosen dishes, it will be a thoughtful expression of your nutritional and culinary goals.

Culinary Crusade: Quick and Efficient Cooking Techniques

At the crossroads of nutrition and gastronomy, time and efficiency are compromised by the desire for tasty and nutritious meals. For those who pursue rigorous physique goals, such as bodybuilders, balancing these elements is a constant challenge.

That is why I will share techniques specially adapted for those committed to a rigorous diet:

Advance Preparation of Ingredients

Imagine this scenario: After an exhausting session of weightlifting, you come home hungry. Your body cries out for nutrients. Now, instead of spending long minutes, even hours, preparing a meal from scratch, you have most of the ingredients ready and on hand. Chicken breasts are already marinated with herbs and spices. The sweet potatoes, peeled and cut, are ready to cook. Your washed and chopped salad greens await in airtight containers. The result? In a matter of minutes, you have a nutritious and delicious dish in front of you.

This approach has multiple advantages:

- With ready-made ingredients, valuable time is freed up for other activities, be it additional training, stretching, or just rest.
- By planning and preparing ahead, you make food decisions with a cool head, choosing what is truly beneficial to your goals. There is no room for impulsive or less healthy choices.
- You reduce the risk of food spoiling. You just have to wash, cut, and store them properly, thus increasing the probability that they will be consumed.
- Having ingredients ready offers a variety of possible combinations. One day, those marinated chicken breasts can go on the grill; the next, they can be cut into strips for quick frying.
- Knowing that when you come home from the gym there are ingredients ready to cook takes a load off your shoulders. Feeding becomes a pleasant experience and not a tedious task.
- You make sure to consume dishes that nourish and align with what your body needs at that specific moment.

Preparing ingredients ahead of time is a cooking technique that is integrated into the journey of transformation, ensuring that your body is always fueled, satisfied, and ready for the next challenge.

High-Temperature Cooking

This technique involves cooking food at temperatures higher than what is commonly used. The result is accelerated cooking that, if done right, retains flavors, juiciness, and, what is most important for the bodybuilder, the valuable nutrients. The benefits and methods of this technique are explored here:

- Proteins, so crucial for muscle building and recovery, remain intact. Minerals and vitamins, which could break down or evaporate during prolonged cooking, remain in the food.
- High-temperature cooking caramelizes the natural sugars in food, intensifying its flavor. This caramelization results in a crisp, golden finish on the outside, while the inside remains juicy.
- Less time cooking means reduced energy use, be it gas or electricity, which in turn is beneficial for the environment and personal finances.
- From lean meats like chicken or turkey to high-fiber vegetables like broccoli or carrots, almost any food benefits from this technique. Fish, in particular, cook to perfection using this method, as its delicate meat remains tender on the inside.
- Less oil or fat is required than other methods. This is particularly useful for bodybuilders looking to reduce fat intake while maximizing protein.

To master cooking at high temperatures, certain recommendations must be taken into account:

- Use pans or saucepans that conduct heat well and can withstand high temperatures. Cast iron or stainless steel are ideal for this purpose.
- Due to high temperatures, it is easy for food to overcook or burn. Food needs to be watched and sometimes moved to ensure even cooking.
- For best results, it is recommended that foods come to room temperature before cooking. This ensures even cooking.

High-temperature cooking is positioned as a culinary technique that perfectly meets the needs of the modern bodybuilder: efficiency, nutrient preservation, and flavor. By integrating it into their culinary repertoire, the bodybuilder equips themselves with a powerful tool that supports their path to physical excellence.

Double Pan Method

The concept behind the double pan method is simple: two pans are used instead of one. But why would anyone want to? The answer lies in the speed and efficiency with which food is cooked. Using two pans, one on top of the other, creates an environment similar to that of an oven but on the stovetop, allowing food to cook evenly on both sides without the need to flip it.

These are the benefits:

- Because they cook faster and in their juices, foods retain more of their nutrients, ensuring that you get the maximum amount of benefit from each ingredient.
- The technique ensures that food is cooked evenly, avoiding raw or overcooked parts. This is useful for proteins like chicken or fish, where proper cooking is crucial for both food safety and optimal texture and flavor.
- Due to cooking in a semi-sealed environment, the need to use large amounts of oils or fats is reduced. This helps bodybuilders maintain a clean nutritional profile and focus on their goals.
- Although it sounds specialized, the method is surprisingly versatile. It can be used to cook a variety of foods, from vegetables to meat and fish.

To employ this technique, two pans are required that fit well one on top of the other. Here is a basic procedure:

Heating: First, heat the lower pan over medium fire, then the food is placed in it and covered with the second pan, ensuring a good seal between the two.

Monitoring: Since food cooks faster, it is important to be vigilant to prevent burning or overcooking. The advantage here is that it is not necessary to turn the food since it is being cooked from the top and bottom simultaneously.

Completion: When the food is cooked to perfection, it is simply removed from the heat and served. If grill marks or a specific texture are desired, the food can be turned at the final stage so that it is in direct contact with the pan.

With the double pan method, you save time, while ensuring perfect cooking and optimal preservation of nutrients.

Always remember that beyond what we eat, it is how we prepare those foods that can make a significant difference. Cooking for bodybuilders is an art unto itself, combining the science of nutrition with culinary skills. Now that you've made it this far, you're well prepared to keep moving forward! Don't stop reading the next chapter!

Chapter 4
Bodybuilding Recipes – Fitness Banquet

Congratulations! You are halfway there and have embarked on a journey that will transform your body and your relationship with food. Now is the time to discover the true taste of bodybuilding-focused nutrition, a world where every bite counts, every ingredient has a purpose, and every recipe is a promise of progress.

This chapter is meticulously designed to offer you several dishes that will please your palate while working in sync with your fitness goals.

Imagine energizing breakfasts that set you up for a day of intense training, balanced lunches that fuel your muscles, and dinners that satisfy your appetite while supporting your recovery. Gone are the days when diet food was synonymous with bland. On the following pages, you'll find delicious and nutritious options that show you that it's possible to enjoy food while pursuing bodybuilding excellence.

Bon appetite and get on with your journey to fitness success!

Sunrise Delights: Power-Packed Breakfast Recipes

Spinach and Feta Cheese Omelet

Preparation time: 10 minutes

Cooking time: 8 minutes

Servings: 2

Ingredients:

» Eggs: 4 (USA) | 4 units (Europe)
» Fresh spinach: 1 cup (USA) | 240 ml (Europe)
» Feta cheese: 1/2 cup (USA) | 120 ml (Europe) (crumbled)
» Olive oil: 1 tbsp (USA) | 15 ml (Europe)
» Salt: 1/4 tsp (USA) | 1.25 ml (Europe)
» Black pepper: 1/8 tsp (USA) | 0.625 ml (Europe)
» Cherry tomatoes: 1/2 cup (USA) | 120 ml (Europe) (optional for garnish)

Preparation:

1. In a large bowl, beat the eggs and add a pinch of salt and pepper. Set aside.
2. Heat the olive oil in a skillet over medium-high fire, then add the fresh spinach and fry until slightly wilted, which will take about 2–3 minutes.
3. Pour the beaten eggs over the spinach in the skillet. Cook, without stirring, until the edges begin to set. Use a spatula to gently lift the edges as you tilt the pan so the raw egg flows underneath. Continue cooking until the center is almost set.
4. Sprinkle crumbled feta over half of the tortilla.
5. Carefully fold the tortilla in half, covering the cheese.
6. Cook for an additional 1–2 minutes or until the cheese begins to melt.
7. Transfer the tortilla to a plate, garnish with cherry tomatoes if desired, and serve immediately.

Nutritional information (per serving): Calories: 320 | Protein: 20 g | Fat: 24 g (Saturated: 8 g) | Carbohydrates: 4 g | Fiber: 1 g | Sugars: 2 g | Sodium: 560 mg.

Oatmeal and Banana Energy Smoothie

Preparation time: 7 minutes

Cooking time: 0 minutes

Servings: 1

Ingredients:

- » Oats: 1/2 cup (USA) | 120 ml (Europe)
- » Ripe banana: 1
- » Protein powder: 1 tbsp (USA) | 30 g (Europe)
- » Almond milk: 1 cup (USA) | 240 ml (Europe)
- » Almonds: 10 units

Preparation:

1. Combine all ingredients in a blender and process until smooth.

Nutritional information (per serving): Calories: 360 | Protein: 28 g | Carbohydrates: 45 g | Fat: 10 g (Saturated: 1 g) | Sugar: 20 g | Sodium: 45 mg | Fiber: 8 g.

Breakfast Burrito With Egg and Black Beans

Preparation time: 25 minutes

Cooking time: 15 minutes

Servings: 2 burritos

Ingredients:

» Eggs: 4
» Cooked black beans: 1/2 cup (USA) | 120 ml (Europe)
» Whole wheat tortillas: 2
» Grated cheddar cheese: 1/4 cup (USA) | 60 ml (Europe)
» Pico de gallo: 1/2 cup (USA) | 120 ml (Europe)

Preparation:

1. Beat the eggs and scramble them in a frying pan.
2. Add the cooked black beans.
3. Heat the tortillas and place the egg and bean mixture in the center.
4. Sprinkle with cheddar cheese and pico de gallo.
5. Roll up and serve hot.

Nutritional information (per serving): Calories: 320 | Protein: 22 g | Fat: 12 g (Saturated: 4 g) | Carbohydrates: 35 g | Fiber: 7 g | Sugars: 3 g | Sodium: 390 mg

Fruit Smoothie With Protein

Preparation time: 10 minutes

Cooking time: 0 minutes

Servings: 2

Ingredients:

- » Protein powder: 2 scoops (USA) | 60 g (Europe)
- » Milk: 1 cup (USA) | 240 ml (Europe)
- » Frozen fruits (mango, pineapple, strawberries): 1 cup (USA) | 240 ml (Europe)

Preparation:

1. Place all the ingredients in a blender.
2. Process until you obtain a smooth and homogeneous mixture.
3. Serve immediately.

Nutritional information (per serving): Calories: 270 | Protein: 25 g | Fat: 2 g (Saturated: 0.5 g) | Carbohydrates: 35 g | Fiber: 4 g | Sugars: 28 g | Sodium: 120 mg

Baked Eggs With Asparagus and Tomatoes

Preparation time: 15 minutes

Cooking time: 20 minutes

Servings: 2

Ingredients:

» Eggs: 4
» Fresh asparagus: 8 stalks
» Cherry tomatoes: 10
» Olive oil: 1 tbsp (USA) | 15 ml (Europe)

Preparation:

1. Preheat the oven to 400 °F (200 °C).
2. In a frying pan, sauté the cut asparagus and cherry tomatoes in olive oil.
3. Place the vegetables in a baking dish. Make room for the eggs and crack them on top.
4. Bake for 15–20 minutes or until the eggs are cooked to your liking.

Nutritional information (per serving): Calories: 210 | Protein: 20 g | Fat: 12 g (Saturated: 3 g) | Carbohydrates: 8 g | Fiber: 3 g | Sugars: 4 g | Sodium: 160 mg

Egg and Turkey Rolls

Preparation time: 15 minutes

Cooking time: 10 minutes

Servings: 2 rolls

Ingredients:

» Eggs: 3
» Cooked and chopped turkey: 3.5 oz (USA) | 100 g (Europe)
» Fresh spinach: 1 cup (USA) | 240 ml (Europe)
» Tomato: 1, chopped
» Olive oil: 1 tbsp (USA) | 15 ml (Europe)

Preparation:

1. Beat the eggs and pour them into a hot pan with a little oil.
2. Add the chopped turkey, spinach, and tomato.
3. Cook until the eggs are set, then roll.
4. Serve hot.

Nutritional information (per serving): Calories: 230 | Protein: 24 g | Fat: 13 g (Saturated: 4 g) | Carbohydrates: 5 g | Fiber: 2 g | Sugars: 2 g | Sodium: 320 mg

Yogurt and Granola Parfait

Preparation time: 15 minutes

Cooking time: 0 minutes

Servings: 2 parfaits

Ingredients:

»   Greek yogurt: 2 cups (USA) | 480 ml (Europe)
»   Granola: 1 cup (USA) | 240 ml (Europe)
»   Honey: 2 tbsp (USA) | 30 ml (Europe)
»   Assorted fruits: 1 cup (USA) | 240 ml (Europe)

Preparation:

1.   In a glass, layer yogurt, granola, fruit, and a small amount of honey.
2.   When the glass is filled, repeat.

Nutritional information (per serving): Calories: 310 | Protein: 20 g | Carbohydrates: 40 g | Fat: 8 g (Saturated: 3 g) | Sugar: 25 g | Sodium: 65 mg | Fiber: 6 g.

Chia and Red Fruit Parfait

Preparation time: 15 minutes

Cooking time: 0 minutes

Servings: 2 parfaits

Ingredients:

- » Chia seeds: 3 tbsp (USA) | 45 ml (Europe)
- » Milk: 1 cup (USA) | 240 ml (Europe)
- » Red fruit: 1 cup (USA) | 240 ml (Europe)
- » Protein powder: 1 tbsp (USA) | 30 g (Europe)

Preparation:

1. Mix chia seeds with milk and protein powder until smooth.
2. Refrigerate for at least 2 hours.
3. When serving, alternate layers of the chia mixture and red fruit.

Nutritional information (per serving): Calories: 260 | Proteins: 21 g | Fat: 8 g (Saturated: 2.5 g) | Carbohydrates: 28 g | Fiber: 10 g | Sugars: 12 g | Sodium: 40 mg

Chickpea Waffles

Preparation time: 20 minutes

Cooking time: 10 minutes

Servings: 2 waffles

Ingredients:

» Chickpea flour: 1 cup (USA) | 240 ml (Europe)
» Eggs: 2
» Milk: 1/2 cup (USA) | 120 ml (Europe)
» Honey: 1 tbsp (USA) | 15 ml (Europe)

Preparation:

1. Combine all the ingredients until you obtain a uniform dough.
2. Cook in a preheated waffle maker until golden brown.
3. Serve with honey or your favorite topping.

Nutritional information (per serving): Calories: 290 | Proteins: 22 g | Fat: 5 g (Saturated: 1 g) | Carbohydrates: 40 g | Fiber: 8 g | Sugars: 6 g | Sodium: 210 mg

Cottage and Fruit Bowl

Preparation time: 10 minutes

Cooking time: 0 minutes

Servings: 2 bowls

Ingredients:

- » Cottage cheese: 1 cup (USA) | 240 ml (Europe)
- » Strawberries: 1/2 cup (USA) | 120 ml (Europe)
- » Kiwi: 1, chopped
- » Chopped walnuts: 1/4 cup (USA) | 60 ml (Europe)

Preparation:

1. In individual bowls, place the cottage cheese, and add the strawberries and kiwi.
2. Decorate with chopped walnuts.

Nutritional information (per serving): Calories: 250 | Proteins: 21 g | Fat: 8 g (Saturated: 3 g) | Carbohydrates: 25 g | Fiber: 4 g | Sugars: 14 g | Sodium: 320 mg

Cottage Bowl With Fruit and Almonds

Preparation time: 10 minutes

Cooking time: 0 minutes

Servings: 2

Ingredients:

» Cottage cheese: 2 cups (USA) | 480 ml (Europe)
» Sliced almonds: 1/4 cup (USA) | 60 ml (Europe)
» Fruit mix (mango, strawberries, kiwi): 1 cup (USA) | 240 ml (Europe)
» Honey: 2 tbsp (USA) | 30 ml (Europe)

Preparation:

1. In a bowl, add the cottage cheese and place the fruit mix and sliced almonds on top.
2. Drizzle honey on top.
3. Stir gently and enjoy.

Nutritional information (per serving): Calories: 320 | Proteins: 27 g | Fat: 12 g (Saturated: 2 g) | Carbohydrates: 30 g | Fiber: 4 g | Sugars: 16 g | Sodium: 340 mg

Chicken and Avocado Wrap

Preparation time: 15 minutes

Cooking time: 10 minutes

Servings: 2 wraps

Ingredients:

» Chicken breast: 7 oz (USA) | 200 g (Europe)
» Ripe avocado: 1
» Whole wheat tortillas: 2
» Chopped romaine lettuce: 1 cup (USA) | 240 ml (Europe)
» Tomato: 1, chopped
» Yogurt or tahini sauce: 2 tbsp (USA) | 30 ml (Europe)
» Olive oil: 1 tbsp (USA) | 15 ml (Europe)
» Salt and pepper to taste

Preparation:

1. Heat the olive oil in a frying pan and cook the chicken breast seasoned with salt and pepper until completely cooked and golden.
2. Once cooked, cut the chicken into thin strips.
3. On a tortilla, place a layer of lettuce, followed by chopped tomato, chicken strips, and avocado slices.
4. Drizzle with yogurt or tahini sauce.
5. Roll the tortilla tightly and cut it in half to serve.

Nutritional information (per serving): Calories: 370 | Proteins: 30 g | Fat: 15 g (Saturated: 2.5 g) | Carbohydrates: 35 g | Fiber: 7 g | Sugars: 4 g | Sodium: 450 mg

Noon Time: High Protein Lunches

Grilled Chicken With Quinoa and Broccoli

Preparation time: 10 minutes

Cooking time: 20 minutes

Servings: 2

Ingredients:

» Chicken (breast without skin): 2 pieces (USA) | 2 pieces (Europe)
» Quinoa: 1 cup (USA) | 240 ml (Europe)
» Broccoli: 2 cups (USA) | 480 ml (Europe) (cut into florets)
» Olive oil: 1 tbsp (USA) | 15 ml (Europe)
» Salt: 1/2 tsp (USA) | 2.5 ml (Europe)
» Black pepper: 1/4 tsp (USA) | 1.25 ml (Europe)
» Garlic powder: 1/4 tsp (USA) | 1.25 ml (Europe)

Preparation:

1. Preheat the grill to a medium-high flame.
2. Season the chicken breasts with salt, pepper, and garlic powder.
3. In a large skillet, heat the olive oil over medium fire. Add the broccoli florets and sauté for 5⊠7 minutes or until glossy-tender. Set aside.
4. Grill the chicken for 6–7 minutes on each side or until cooked through.
5. While the chicken is cooking, in a small saucepan, bring 2 cups of water to a boil. Add the quinoa and reduce the heat to low. Cook covered for 15 minutes or until the quinoa is tender.
6. Serve the grilled chicken along with the quinoa and broccoli stir-fry.

Nutritional information (per serving): Calories: 420 | Protein: 40 g | Fat: 12 g (Saturated: 2 g) | Carbohydrates: 40 g | Fiber: 5 g | Sugars: 2 g | Sodium: 650 mg.

Baked Salmon With Chickpea Salad

Preparation time: 15 minutes

Cooking time: 15 minutes

Servings: 2

Ingredients:

» Salmon: 2 fillets (USA) | 2 pieces (Europe)
» Cooked chickpeas: 1 cup (USA) | 240 ml (Europe)
» Cherry tomatoes: 1/2 cup (USA) | 120 ml (Europe) (halved)
» Cucumber: 1/2 (USA) | 1/2 unit (Europe) (chopped)
» Red onion: 1/4 (USA) | 1/4 unit (Europe) (finely chopped)
» Olive oil: 2 tbsp (USA) | 30 ml (Europe)
» Lemon juice: 1 tbsp (USA) | 15 ml (Europe)
» Dried dill: 1/2 tsp (USA) | 2.5 ml (Europe)
» Salt: 1/4 tsp (USA) | 1.25 ml (Europe)
» Black pepper: 1/4 tsp (USA) | 1.25 ml (Europe)

Preparation:

1. Preheat the oven to 375°F (190°C).
2. Place the salmon fillets on a baking tray. Drizzle with 1 tbsp of olive oil, salt, pepper, and dill. Bake for 12–15 minutes or until the salmon falls apart easily with a fork.
3. While the salmon is cooking, in a large bowl, combine the chickpeas, cherry tomatoes, cucumber, red onion, lemon juice, and the remaining tablespoon of olive oil. Mix well and season with salt and pepper to taste.
4. Serve the baked salmon accompanied by the chickpea salad.

Nutritional information (per serving): Calories: 465 | Protein: 35 g | Fat: 25 g (Saturated: 4 g) | Carbohydrates: 30 g | Fiber: 8 g | Sugars: 5 g | Sodium: 320 mg.

Asian-Style Beef With Broccoli

Preparation time: 15 minutes

Cooking time: 10 minutes

Servings: 2

Ingredients:

» Veal (lean fillet): 8 oz. (USA) | 225 g (Europe) (cut into strips)
» Broccoli: 2 cups (USA) | 480 ml (Europe) (cut into florets)
» Sesame oil: 1 tbsp (USA) | 15 ml (Europe)
» Soy sauce: 2 tbsp (USA) | 30 ml (Europe)
» Garlic: 2 cloves (USA) | 2 units (Europe) (minced)
» Fresh ginger: 1/2 inch (USA) | 1.25 cm (Europe) (grated)
» Sesame seeds: 1 tsp (USA) | 5 ml (Europe) (for garnish)

Preparation:

1. Heat the sesame oil in a large skillet or wok over medium-high fire.
2. Add the garlic and grated ginger, sautéing until fragrant (about 30 seconds).
3. Add the shredded beef and fry until well browned.
4. Add the broccoli florets and soy sauce. Stir well and cook until the broccoli is tender and the veal is cooked through.
5. Serve hot and sprinkle with sesame seeds.

Nutritional information (per serving): Calories: 320 | Protein: 30 g | Fat: 14 g (Saturated: 3 g) | Carbohydrates: 20 g | Fiber: 4 g | Sugars: 3 g | Sodium: 920 mg.

Lentils With Spinach and Hard-Boiled Egg

Preparation time: 10 minutes

Cooking time: 30 minutes

Servings: 2

Ingredients:

- » Lentils: 1 cup (USA) | 240 ml (Europe) (washed and drained)
- » Fresh spinach: 2 cups (USA) | 480 ml (Europe)
- » Eggs: 2 (USA) | 2 units (Europe)
- » Olive oil: 1 tbsp (USA) | 15 ml (Europe)
- » Salt: 1/4 tsp (USA) | 1.25 ml (Europe)
- » Black pepper: 1/8 tsp (USA) | 0.625 ml (Europe)
- » Onion: 1/2 (USA) | 1/2 unit (Europe) (finely chopped)

Preparation:

1. In a saucepan, bring 3 cups of water to a boil. Add the lentils, lower the heat, and simmer for 25 minutes or until tender. Drain off excess water.
2. While the lentils are cooking, in another saucepan, bring water to a boil and cook the eggs for 10 minutes. Cool, peel, and reserve.
3. In a skillet, heat the olive oil and fry the onion until transparent. Add the spinach and cook until wilted.
4. Mix the cooked lentils with the spinach and onion. Season with salt and pepper.
5. Serve the lentils with spinach on a plate and place a hard-boiled egg on top.

Nutritional information (per serving): Calories: 380 | Protein: 25 g | Fat: 10 g (Saturated: 2 g) | Carbohydrates: 50 g | Fiber: 20 g | Sugars: 3 g | Sodium: 320 mg.

Turkey Meatballs

Preparation time: 15 minutes

Cooking time: 20 minutes

Servings: 2

Ingredients:

» Ground turkey: 1/2 lb (USA) | 225 g (Europe)
» Breadcrumbs: 1/4 cup (USA) | 60 ml (Europe)
» Egg: 1 (USA) | 1 unit (Europe)
» Garlic: 1 clove (USA) | 1 unit (Europe) (minced)
» Fresh parsley: 1 tbsp (USA) | 15 ml (Europe) (chopped)
» Salt: 1/4 tsp (USA) | 1.25 ml (Europe)
» Black pepper: 1/8 tsp (USA) | 0.625 ml (Europe)
» Ketchup: 1 cup (USA) | 240 ml (Europe)
» Olive oil: 1 tbsp (USA) | 15 ml (Europe)

Preparation:

1. In a bowl, mix the ground turkey, breadcrumbs, egg, garlic, parsley, salt, and pepper. Shape small meatballs with the mixture.
2. Heat the olive oil in a large skillet over medium fire. Add the meatballs and fry until golden brown on all sides.
3. Pour the tomato sauce over the meatballs, reduce the heat to low, and simmer for 10 minutes.
4. Serve hot.

Nutritional information (per serving): Calories: 350 | Protein: 30 g | Fat: 15 g (Saturated: 3 g) | Carbohydrates: 25 g | Fiber: 3 g | Sugars: 5 g | Sodium: 720 mg.

Whole Wheat Pasta With Tuna and Arugula

Preparation time: 10 minutes

Cooking time: 15 minutes

Servings: 2

Ingredients:

» Whole wheat pasta (penne or fusilli): 1 cup (USA) | 240 ml (Europe)
» Canned Tuna (plain): 1 can (USA) | 1 can (Europe) (drained)
» Arugula: 2 cups (USA) | 480 ml (Europe)
» Cherry tomatoes: 1/2 cup (USA) | 120 ml (Europe) (halved)
» Olive oil: 2 tbsp (USA) | 30 ml (Europe)
» Lemon juice: 1 tbsp (USA) | 15 ml (Europe)
» Salt: 1/4 tsp (USA) | 1.25 ml (Europe)
» Black pepper: 1/8 tsp (USA) | 0.625 ml (Europe)

Preparation:

1. Cook the whole wheat pasta according to package directions until al dente. Drain and reserve.
2. In a large bowl, combine the cooked pasta, drained tuna, arugula, and cherry tomatoes.
3. In a small bowl, mix the olive oil, lemon juice, salt, and pepper. Pour the dressing over the pasta and mix well.
4. Serve immediately.

Nutritional information (per serving): Calories: 430 | Protein: 30 g | Fat: 12 g (Saturated: 2 g) | Carbohydrates: 55 g | Fiber: 8 g | Sugars: 4 g | Sodium: 420 mg.

Grilled Chicken With Quinoa and Vegetables

Preparation time: 15 minutes

Cooking time: 20 minutes

Servings: 2

Ingredients:

» Chicken breast: 2 (USA) | 2 units (Europe)
» Quinoa: 1/2 cup (USA) | 120 ml (Europe)
» Broccoli: 1 cup (USA) | 240 ml (Europe) (florets)
» Carrots: 2 (USA) | 2 (Europe) (peeled and thinly sliced)
» Garlic: 1 clove (USA) | 1 unit (Europe) (minced)
» Olive oil: 2 tbsp (USA) | 30 ml (Europe)
» Lemon: 1/2 (USA) | 1/2 unit (Europe) (juice)
» Salt: 1/4 tsp (USA) | 1.25 ml (Europe)
» Black pepper: 1/8 tsp (USA) | 0.625 ml (Europe)

Preparation:

1. Cook the quinoa according to the package instructions. Drain and reserve.
2. In a large skillet, heat a tablespoon of olive oil over medium fire. Add the minced garlic, broccoli, and carrots. Sauté the vegetables until tender.
3. Add the cooked quinoa to the pan and mix well. Season with salt and pepper.
4. On a grill or skillet, cook the chicken breasts with a tablespoon of olive oil until golden brown.
5. Serve the chicken breasts along with the quinoa and vegetable mixture. Drizzle with lemon juice.

Nutritional information (per serving): Calories: 410 | Protein: 40 g | Fat: 12 g (Saturated: 2 g) | Carbohydrates: 35 g | Fiber: 5 g | Sugars: 3 g | Sodium: 320 mg.

Baked Salmon With Brussels Sprouts and Almonds

Preparation time: 15 minutes

Cooking time: 20 minutes

Servings: 2

Ingredients:

» Salmon: 2 fillets (USA) | 2 pieces (Europe)
» Brussels sprouts: 1 cup (USA) | 240 ml (Europe) (clean and halved)
» Almonds: 1/4 cup (USA) | 60 ml (Europe) (chopped)
» Olive oil: 2 tbsp (USA) | 30 ml (Europe)
» Salt: 1/4 tsp (USA) | 1.25 ml (Europe)
» Black pepper: 1/8 tsp (USA) | 0.625 ml (Europe)
» Lemon: 1/2 (USA) | 1/2 unit (Europe) (juice and zest)

Preparation:

1. Preheat the oven to 400°F (200°C).
2. Place the salmon fillets on a baking sheet. Drizzle with half the olive oil, lemon juice, lemon zest, salt, and pepper.
3. In a bowl, mix the Brussels sprouts with the remaining olive oil, salt, and pepper. Add to the pan around the salmon.
4. Bake for 15–20 minutes or until the salmon is well cooked and the sprouts are tender.
5. Serve the salmon and Brussels sprouts on plates and sprinkle with chopped almonds.

Nutritional information (per serving): Calories: 400 | Protein: 35 g | Fat: 25 g (Saturated: 4 g) | Carbohydrates: 15 g | Fiber: 5 g | Sugars: 3 g | Sodium: 320 mg.

Chickpea Salad With Chicken and Avocado

Preparation time: 15 minutes

Cooking time: 0 minutes (if you use already cooked chicken)

Servings: 2

Ingredients:

» Cooked chickpeas: 1 cup (USA) | 240 ml (Europe) (rinsed and drained)
» Cooked chicken breast: 1 (USA) | 1 (Europe) (shredded)
» Avocado: 1 (USA) | 1 unit (Europe) (peeled and chopped)
» Tomato: 1 (USA) | 1 unit (Europe) (chopped)
» Red onion: 1/4 (USA) | 1/4 unit (Europe) (finely chopped)
» Lemon juice: 2 tbsp (USA) | 30 ml (Europe)
» Olive oil: 2 tbsp (USA) | 30 ml (Europe)
» Salt: 1/4 tsp (USA) | 1.25 ml (Europe)
» Black pepper: 1/8 tsp (USA) | 0.625 ml (Europe)

Preparation:

1. In a large bowl, combine the chickpeas, shredded chicken, avocado, tomato, and red onion.
2. In a small bowl, combine the lemon juice, olive oil, salt, and pepper. Mix well and pour over the salad.
3. After thoroughly combining everything, serve.

Nutritional information (per serving): Calories: 440 | Protein: 30 g | Fat: 25 g (Saturated: 4 g) | Carbohydrates: 30 g | Fiber: 10 g | Sugars: 5 g | Sodium: 320 mg.

Turkey in Honey Mustard Sauce

Preparation time: 10 minutes

Cooking time: 15 minutes

Servings: 2

Ingredients:

» Turkey Breast: 8 oz. (USA) | 225 g (Europe) (cut into fillets)
» Dijon mustard: 3 tbsp (USA) | 45 ml (Europe)
» Honey: 1 tbsp (USA) | 15 ml (Europe)
» Olive oil: 1 tbsp (USA) | 15 ml (Europe)
» Fresh rosemary: 1 tsp (USA) | 5 ml (Europe) (chopped)
» Salt: 1/4 tsp (USA) | 1.25 ml (Europe)
» Black pepper: 1/8 tsp (USA) | 0.625 ml (Europe)

Preparation:

1. Combine the mustard, honey, rosemary, salt, and pepper in a small bowl.
2. In a big pan, heat the olive oil over medium-high heat.
3. Add the turkey fillets and cook for 3 to 4 minutes on each side, depending on how done you want your meat.
4. Lower the heat to medium, then stir in the honey mustard mixture in the skillet. Cook the turkey with the sauce on top for 2 to 3 minutes.
5. Serve hot.

Nutritional information (per serving): Calories: 320 | Protein: 40 g | Fat: 10 g (Saturated: 2 g) | Carbohydrates: 20 g | Fiber: 0 g | Sugars: 18 g | Sodium: 720 mg.

Grilled Tuna With Quinoa Salad

Preparation time: 15 minutes

Cooking time: 10 minutes

Servings: 2

Ingredients:

» Fresh Tuna Loin: 8 oz. (USA) | 225 g (Europe)
» Quinoa: 1/2 cup (USA) | 120 ml (Europe) (cooked)
» Red bell pepper: 1/2 (USA) | 1/2 unit (Europe) (chopped)
» Cucumber: 1/2 (USA) | 1/2 unit (Europe) (chopped)
» Black olives: 1/4 cup (USA) | 60 ml (Europe)
» Olive oil: 2 tbsp (USA) | 30 ml (Europe)
» Lemon juice: 1 tbsp (USA) | 15 ml (Europe)
» Salt: 1/4 tsp (USA) | 1.25 ml (Europe)
» Black pepper: 1/8 tsp (USA) | 0.625 ml (Europe)

Preparation:

1. Heat a medium-high flame on the grill. Add pepper and salt to the tuna.
2. Grill the tuna for two to three minutes per side, or until it is cooked to your preference.
3. Combine the quinoa, red bell pepper, cucumber, and black olives in a large bowl.
4. Combine the olive oil, lemon juice, salt, and pepper in a small bowl. Mix thoroughly after pouring over the quinoa salad.
5. Spoon the quinoa salad alongside the grilled tuna.

Nutritional information (per serving): Calories: 420 | Protein: 40 g | Fat: 20 g (Saturated: 3 g) | Carbohydrates: 30 g | Fiber: 4 g | Sugars: 3 g | Sodium: 400 mg.

Grilled Chicken With Sweet Potatoes and Asparagus

Preparation time: 15 minutes

Cooking time: 20 minutes

Servings: 2

Ingredients:

» Skinless chicken breasts: 12 oz. (USA) | 340 g (Europe)
» Sweet potatoes: 1 large (USA) | 1 piece (Europe) (peeled and cut into thick slices)
» Fresh asparagus: 10 stalks (USA) | 10 units (Europe) (ends trimmed)
» Olive oil: 2 tbsp (USA) | 30 ml (Europe)
» Salt: 1/2 tsp (USA) | 2.5 ml (Europe)
» Black pepper: 1/4 tsp (USA) | 1.25 ml (Europe)
» Garlic powder: 1/4 tsp (USA) | 1.25 ml (Europe)
» Paprika: 1/4 tsp (USA) | 1.25 ml (Europe)

Preparation:

1. Light a medium-high flame on the grill.
2. While the chicken is cooking, season the breasts with salt, pepper, paprika, and garlic powder.
3. Sprinkle a little salt and pepper on top of the sweet potato slices and asparagus after brushing with olive oil.
4. Arrange the veggies and chicken on the grill. Cook the chicken until thoroughly done, about 6-7 minutes per side. Cook the asparagus for two minutes on each side then the sweet potatoes for four minutes each.
5. Arrange the sweet potatoes and asparagus on the side and serve the chicken hot.

Nutritional information (per serving): Calories: 440 | Protein: 50 g | Fat: 14 g (Saturated: 2 g) | Carbohydrates: 30 g | Fiber: 6 g | Sugars: 8 g | Sodium: 680 mg.

Baked Salmon With Mediterranean Chickpea Salad

Preparation time: 20 minutes

Cooking time: 15 minutes

Servings: 2

Ingredients:

- » Salmon fillets: 12 oz. (USA) | 340 g (Europe)
- » Cooked chickpeas: 1 cup (USA) | 240 ml (Europe)
- » Cucumber: 1/2 (USA) | 1/2 unit (Europe) (chopped)
- » Cherry tomatoes: 1/2 cup (USA) | 120 ml (Europe) (halved)
- » Red onion: 1/4 (USA) | 1/4 unit (Europe) (finely chopped)
- » Feta cheese: 1/4 cup (USA) | 60 ml (Europe) (crumbled)
- » Olive oil: 2 tbsp (USA) | 30 ml (Europe)
- » Lemon juice: 1 tbsp (USA) | 15 ml (Europe)
- » Dried oregano: 1/2 tsp (USA) | 2.5 ml (Europe)
- » Salt: 1/4 tsp (USA) | 1.25 ml (Europe)
- » Black pepper: 1/8 tsp (USA) | 0.625 ml (Europe)

Preparation:

1. Set the oven temperature to 375°F (190°C).
2. Place the salmon fillets in a single layer on a baking sheet. Sprinkle with salt and pepper. Bake for 12 to 15 minutes or until the salmon flakes easily with a fork.
3. Prepare the chickpea, cucumber, cherry tomato, red onion, and feta salad while the salmon is cooking.
4. Combine olive oil, lemon juice, oregano, salt, and pepper in a small bowl. Mix thoroughly after pouring over the chickpea salad.
5. Put the chickpea salad on the side and serve the baked salmon.

Nutritional information (per serving): Calories: 520 | Protein: 46 g | Fat: 28 g (Saturated: 6 g) | Carbohydrates: 30 g | Fiber: 8 g | Sugars: 6 g | Sodium: 580 mg.

Night Time Nutrition: Healthy and Nutritious Dinners

Grilled Turkey With Roasted Vegetables

Preparation time: 10 minutes

Cooking time: 20 minutes

Servings: 2

Ingredients:

» Turkey breast: 12 oz. (USA) | 340 g (Europe)
» Red bell peppers: 1 (USA) | 1 unit (Europe) (cut into strips)
» Broccoli: 2 cups (USA) | 480 ml (Europe) (florets)
» Olive oil: 2 tbsp (USA) | 30 ml (Europe)
» Salt: 1/2 tsp (USA) | 2.5 ml (Europe)
» Black pepper: 1/4 tsp (USA) | 1.25 ml (Europe)
» Garlic powder: 1/4 tsp (USA) | 1.25 ml (Europe)

Preparation:

1. Turn the grill's heat to medium.
2. Use half the olive oil, salt, pepper, and garlic powder to season the turkey breast.
3. Combine the broccoli and bell peppers with the remaining olive oil, salt, and pepper in a large bowl.
4. To completely cook the turkey, grill it for 6–7 minutes on each side.
5. Grill the veggies until they are soft, about 4–5 minutes, turning them once.
6. Arrange the veggies on the side and serve the turkey.
7. Serve the turkey with the vegetables on the side.

Nutritional information (per serving): Calories: 375 | Protein: 42 g | Fat: 14 g (Saturated fat: 2 g) | Carbohydrates: 16 g | Fiber: 5 g | Sugars: 6 g | Sodium: 650 mg.

Sautéed Tofu With Sesame and Vegetables

Preparation time: 15 minutes

Cooking time: 10 minutes

Servings: 2

Ingredients:

» Firm tofu: 8 oz. (USA) | 227 g (Europe) (drained and cubed)
» Sesame oil: 2 tbsp (USA) | 30 ml (Europe)
» Low sodium soy sauce: 2 tbsp (USA) | 30 ml (Europe)
» Bamboo shoots: 1/2 cup (USA) | 120 ml (Europe)
» Fresh spinach: 2 cups (USA) | 480 ml (Europe)
» Carrot: 1 (USA) | 1 (Europe) (peeled and thinly sliced)
» Sesame seeds: 1 tbsp (USA) | 15 ml (Europe) (toasted)

Preparation:

1. Place a large pan over medium heat and add the sesame oil.
2. Add the tofu and cook for 4-5 minutes, or until browned on both sides.
3. Add the carrot and the bamboo stalks, and sauté for two to three minutes.
4. Once the spinach has wilted, add it along with the soy sauce.
5. Top with sesame seeds and serve warm.

Nutritional information (per serving): Calories: 280 | Protein: 20 g | Fat: 16 g (Saturated: 2.5 g) | Carbohydrates: 15 g | Fiber: 4 g | Sugars: 5 g | Sodium: 450 mg.

Tuna Salad With Avocado and Tomato

Preparation time: 10 minutes

Cooking time: 0 minutes

Servings: 2

Ingredients:

» Canned tuna (plain): 6 oz. (USA) | 170 g (Europe) (drained)
» Avocado: 1 (USA) | 1 (Europe) (peeled, pitted and diced)
» Cherry tomatoes: 1 cup (USA) | 240 ml (Europe) (halved)
» Red onion: 1/4 (USA) | 1/4 unit (Europe) (finely chopped)
» Lemon juice: 1 tbsp (USA) | 15 ml (Europe)
» Olive oil: 2 tbsp (USA) | 30 ml (Europe)
» Salt: 1/4 tsp (USA) | 1.25 ml (Europe)
» Black pepper: 1/8 tsp (USA) | 0.625 ml (Europe)

Preparation:

1. Combine the tuna, avocado, cherry tomatoes, and red onion in a big bowl.
2. Combine the lemon juice, olive oil, salt, and pepper in a small bowl. Stir thoroughly after pouring over the salad.
3. Serve immediately.

Nutritional information (per serving): Calories: 380 | Protein: 25 g | Fat: 26 g (Saturated: 3.5 g) | Carbohydrates: 14 g | Fiber: 8 g | Sugars: 3 g | Sodium: 380 mg.

Teriyaki Chicken With Broccoli

Preparation time: 10 minutes

Cooking time: 15 minutes

Servings: 2

Ingredients:

» Chicken breasts: 10 oz. (USA) | 283 g (Europe) (skinless and boneless)
» Teriyaki sauce: 1/4 cup (USA) | 60 ml (Europe)
» Broccoli: 2 cups (USA) | 480 ml (Europe) (florets)
» Olive oil: 1 tbsp (USA) | 15 ml (Europe)
» Sesame seeds: 1 tbsp (USA) | 15 ml (Europe) (toasted)
» Chives: 1 (USA) | 1 unit (Europe) (chopped)

Preparation:

1. Over a medium flame, warm the olive oil in a large pan.
2. After adding the chicken breasts, fry them for 5-6 minutes on each side, or until they are golden brown and cooked to your preferred doneness.
3. Cover the chicken with the teriyaki sauce and simmer for an additional two to three minutes.
4. Boil the broccoli for 4-5 minutes, or until crisp-tender, while the chicken is cooking.
5. Garnish the hot chicken with sesame seeds, chives, and broccoli on the side.

Nutritional information (per serving): Calories: 390 | Protein: 40 g | Fat: 12 g (Saturated: 2 g) | Carbohydrates: 26 g | Fiber: 4 g | Sugars: 10 g | Sodium: 900 mg.

Zucchini Spaghetti With Turkey Meatballs

Preparation time: 15 minutes

Cooking time: 25 minutes

Servings: 2

Ingredients:

- » Ground turkey: 8 oz. (USA) | 227 g (Europe)
- » Zucchini: 2 (USA) | 2 (Europe) (turned into spaghetti with a vegetable grater)
- » Garlic: 2 cloves (USA) | 2 cloves (Europe) (minced)
- » Low sodium ketchup: 1 cup (USA) | 240 ml (Europe)
- » Grated Parmesan cheese: 2 tbsp (USA) | 30 ml (Europe)
- » Fresh basil: 1/4 cup (USA) | 60 ml (Europe) (chopped)
- » Salt: 1/4 tsp (USA) | 1.25 ml (Europe)
- » Black pepper: 1/8 tsp (USA) | 0.625 ml (Europe)

Preparation:

1. Use the ground turkey to form little meatballs. Set aside.
2. In a large skillet, add the minced garlic and cook until golden.
3. Add the meatballs and heat until well-done or until golden brown, whichever comes first.
4. Include the tomato sauce and simmer for 10 minutes.
5. Sauté the spaghetti made from zucchini for 3 to 4 minutes, or until it just begins to soften.
6. Arrange the meatballs over the spaghetti made from zucchini and top with basil and Parmesan cheese.

Nutritional information (per serving): Calories: 380 | Protein: 35 g | Fat: 14 g (Saturated: 3 g) | Carbohydrates: 28 g | Fiber: 6 g | Sugars: 12 g | Sodium: 520 mg.

Grilled Salmon With Asparagus

Preparation time: 10 minutes

Cooking time: 12 minutes

Servings: 2

Ingredients:

» Salmon: 12 oz. (USA) | 340 g (Europe) (2 fillets)
» Asparagus: 10 stems (USA) | 10 stems (Europe)
» Lemon: 1 (USA) | 1 unit (Europe) (sliced)
» Olive oil: 2 tbsp (USA) | 30 ml (Europe)
» Salt: 1/4 tsp (USA) | 1.25 ml (Europe)
» Black pepper: 1/8 tsp (USA) | 0.625 ml (Europe)

Preparation:

1. Add 1 tbsp of olive oil to a pan that is already hot over a medium-high flame.
2. Add a couple of lemon wedges, salt, and pepper to the fish.
3. Depending on how done you want the salmon, cook it in the pan for 5–6 minutes on each side, until golden.
4. In another pan, add the remaining olive oil and sauté the asparagus for 4⊠5 minutes, or until tender.
5. Serve the salmon hot along with the asparagus.

Nutritional information (per serving): Calories: 370 | Protein: 35 g | Fat: 22 g (Saturated: 4 g) | Carbohydrates: 5 g | Fiber: 2 g | Sugars: 2 g | Sodium: 360 mg.

Chicken Fajitas

Preparation time: 15 minutes

Cooking time: 20 minutes

Servings: 2

Ingredients:

» Chicken breast: 10 oz. (USA) | 283 g (Europe) (Strips)
» Red bell pepper: 1 (USA) | 1 unit (Europe) (striped)
» Green bell pepper: 1 (USA) | 1 unit (Europe) (in strips)
» Onion: 1 (USA) | 1 unit (Europe) (thinly sliced)
» Whole wheat tortillas: 4 (USA) | 4 units (Europe)
» Olive oil: 1 tbsp (USA) | 15 ml (Europe)
» Salt: 1/4 tsp (USA) | 1.25 ml (Europe)
» Black pepper: 1/8 tsp (USA) | 0.625 ml (Europe)

Preparation:

1. In a large skillet, heat the olive oil and add the chicken. Cook until golden.
2. Add the bell peppers and onion, and season with salt and pepper. Cook until the vegetables are tender.
3. Heat the tortillas in another skillet or the microwave.
4. Serve the chicken and vegetables on the tortillas and fold like a fajita.

Nutritional information (per serving): Calories: 450 | Protein: 40 g | Fat: 12 g (Saturated: 3 g) | Carbohydrates: 50 g | Fiber: 8 g | Sugars: 7 g | Sodium: 520 mg.

Beef Steak With Mushrooms

Preparation time: 10 minutes

Cooking time: 15 minutes

Servings: 2

Ingredients:

» Beef steak: 12 oz. (USA) | 340 g (Europe)
» Mushrooms: 1 cup (USA) | 240 ml (Europe) (sliced)
» Garlic: 2 cloves (USA) | 2 cloves (Europe) (minced)
» Olive oil: 2 tbsp (USA) | 30 ml (Europe)
» Salt: 1/4 tsp (USA) | 1.25 ml (Europe)
» Black pepper: 1/8 tsp (USA) | 0.625 ml (Europe)

Preparation:

1. Heat 1 tbsp of olive oil in a skillet over a medium-high fire. Add the beef steak seasoned with salt and pepper. Cook to your preference.
2. In another pan, heat the remaining olive oil and add the garlic and mushrooms. Sauté until the mushrooms are golden.
3. Serve the steak hot accompanied by the mushrooms.

Nutritional information (per serving): Calories: 450 | Protein: 40 g | Fat: 28 g (Saturated: 10 g) | Carbohydrates: 5 g | Fiber: 1 g | Sugars: 2 g | Sodium: 380 mg.

Garlic Shrimp With Broccoli

Preparation time: 10 minutes

Cooking time: 10 minutes

Servings: 2

Ingredients:

- » Shrimp: 12 oz. (USA) | 340 g (Europe) (peeled and deveined)
- » Broccoli: 2 cups (USA) | 480 ml (Europe) (florets)
- » Garlic: 3 cloves (USA) | 3 cloves (Europe) (minced)
- » Olive oil: 2 tbsp (USA) | 30 ml (Europe)
- » Lemon: 1/2 (USA) | 1/2 unit (Europe) (squeezed)
- » Salt: 1/4 tsp (USA) | 1.25 ml (Europe)
- » Black pepper: 1/8 tsp (USA) | 0.625 ml (Europe)

Preparation:

1. Heat 1 tbsp of olive oil in a large skillet over a medium-high flame. Add the broccoli and season with salt. Cook until tender, about 5 minutes.
2. In another pan, heat the remaining olive oil and add the garlic. Sauté for 1 minute.
3. Add the shrimp to the garlic, and season with salt, pepper, and lemon juice. Cook until the shrimp are pink, about 2–3 minutes per side.
4. Serve the garlic shrimp with the broccoli.

Nutritional information (per serving): Calories: 310 | Protein: 40 g | Fat: 12 g (Saturated: 2 g) | Carbohydrates: 10 g | Fiber: 3 g | Sugars: 2 g | Sodium: 380 mg.

Teriyaki Tofu With Brown Rice

Preparation time: 15 minutes

Cooking time: 20 minutes

Servings: 2

Ingredients:

» Tofu: 10 oz. (USA) | 283 g (Europe) (diced)
» Brown rice: 1 cup (USA) | 240 ml (Europe) (cooked)
» Teriyaki sauce: 1/4 cup (USA) | 60 ml (Europe)
» Sesame oil: 1 tbsp (USA) | 15 ml (Europe)
» Green onion: 2 (USA) | 2 (Europe) (chopped)
» Sesame: 1 tbsp (USA) | 15 ml (Europe)

Preparation:

1. Heat the sesame oil in a skillet over a medium flame.
2. Add the tofu and cook until golden on all sides.
3. Reduce the heat and add the teriyaki sauce. Let cook for 5 minutes, until the tofu is well coated and caramelized.
4. Top the brown rice with the teriyaki tofu and top with sesame seeds and green onions.

Nutritional information (per serving): Calories: 450 | Protein: 25 g | Fat: 15 g (Saturated: 2.5 g) | Carbohydrates: 60 g | Fiber: 4 g | Sugars: 5 g | Sodium: 530 mg.

Turkey Meatballs With Tomato Sauce

Preparation time: 15 minutes

Cooking time: 20 minutes

Servings: 2

Ingredients:

» Ground turkey meat: 10 oz. (USA) | 283 g (Europe)
» Crushed tomato: 1 cup (USA) | 240 ml (Europe)
» Garlic: 2 cloves (USA) | 2 cloves (Europe) (minced)
» Oregano: 1 tsp (USA) | 5 ml (Europe)
» Basil: 1 tsp (USA) | 5 ml (Europe)
» Breadcrumbs: 1/4 cup (USA) | 60 ml (Europe)
» Egg: 1 (USA) | 1 unit (Europe)
» Olive oil: 1 tbsp (USA) | 15 ml (Europe)
» Salt: 1/4 tsp (USA) | 1.25 ml (Europe)
» Black pepper: 1/8 tsp (USA) | 0.625 ml (Europe)

Preparation:

1. In a large bowl, combine the minced turkey, breadcrumbs, egg, salt, pepper, oregano, and basil. Mix well and form small meatballs.
2. Heat the olive oil in a large skillet over a medium flame. Add the meatballs and brown on all sides.
3. Add the minced garlic and fry for 1 minute.
4. Add the crushed tomato, lower the heat, and cook for 15 minutes, until the meatballs are well cooked and the sauce has reduced.
5. Serve hot.

Nutritional information (per serving): Calories: 400 | Protein: 35 g | Fat: 20 g (Saturated: 4.5 g) | Carbohydrates: 25 g | Fiber: 5 g | Sugars: 6 g | Sodium: 490 mg.

Tuna Salad With Avocado

Preparation time: 10 minutes

Cooking time: 0 minutes

Servings: 2

Ingredients:

» Canned tuna: 6 oz. (USA) | 170 g (Europe) (drained)
» Avocado: 1 (USA) | 1 unit (Europe) (chopped)
» Tomato: 1 (USA) | 1 unit (Europe) (chopped)
» Red onion: 1/4 (USA) | 1/4 unit (Europe) (finely chopped)
» Lemon: 1 (USA) | 1 unit (Europe) (squeezed)
» Olive oil: 1 tbsp (USA) | 15 ml (Europe)
» Salt: 1/4 tsp (USA) | 1.25 ml (Europe)
» Black pepper: 1/8 tsp (USA) | 0.625 ml (Europe)

Preparation:

1. Combine the drained tuna, diced avocado, tomato, and red onion in a big bowl.
2. Add lemon juice, olive oil, salt, and pepper. Mix well until all ingredients are well combined.
3. Assemble a fresh salad and serve right away.

Nutritional information (per serving): Calories: 350 | Protein: 25 g | Fat: 22 g (Saturated: 3.5 g) | Carbohydrates: 15 g | Fiber: 8 g | Sugars: 4 g | Sodium: 370 mg.

Baked Salmon With Broccoli and Almonds

Preparation time: 15 minutes

Cooking time: 20 minutes

Servings: 2

Ingredients:

- » Salmon: 2 fillets (about 5 oz/150 g each)
- » Broccoli: 2 cups (USA) | 480 ml (Europe) (cut into florets)
- » Flaked almonds: 1/4 cup (USA) | 60 ml (Europe)
- » Garlic: 2 cloves (chopped)
- » Olive oil: 2 tbsp (USA) | 30 ml (Europe)
- » Salt: 1/4 tsp (USA) | 1.25 ml (Europe)
- » Black pepper: 1/8 tsp (USA) | 0.625 ml (Europe)
- » Lemon juice: 1 lemon

Preparation:

1. Preheat oven to 375 °F (190 °C).
2. On a baking sheet, place the salmon fillets and surround them with the broccoli florets.
3. Drizzle with olive oil and season with minced garlic, salt, and pepper.
4. Bake for 15–20 minutes, or until the salmon is cooked through and the broccoli is tender.
5. Remove from the oven and drizzle with lemon juice. Sprinkle the flaked almonds on top before serving.

Nutritional information (per serving): Calories: 400 | Proteins: 35 g | Fat: 22 g (Saturated: 4 g) | Carbohydrates: 12 g | Fiber: 5 g | Sugars: 3 g | Sodium: 330 mg

Managing Hunger: Snacks and Mini-Meals

Turkey and Cheese Wraps

Preparation time: 10 minutes

Cooking time: 0 minutes

Servings: 2

Ingredients:

» Whole wheat tortillas: 2 (USA) | 2 units (Europe)
» Turkey (deli meat): 7 oz (USA) | 200 g (Europe)
» Low-fat cheese: 1.7 oz (USA) | 50 g (Europe)
» Lettuce: 1 cup (USA) | 240 ml (Europe)
» Tomato: 1 (USA) | 1 unit (Europe) (chopped)

Preparation:

1. Place the turkey slices on the tortillas.
2. Add cheese, lettuce, and tomato.
3. Roll up and serve.

Nutritional information (per serving): Calories: 290 | Proteins: 22 g | Fat: 7 g (Saturated: 2.5 g) | Carbohydrates: 30 g | Fiber: 4 g | Sugars: 5 g | Sodium: 1100 mg

Strawberry and Almond Protein Smoothie

Preparation time: 5 minutes

Cooking time: 0 minutes

Servings: 2

Ingredients:

- » Almond milk: 1 cup (USA) | 240 ml (Europe)
- » Protein powder: 2 tbsp (USA) | 60 g (Europe)
- » Strawberries: 1/2 cup (USA) | 120 ml (Europe)
- » Almond butter: 1 tbsp (USA) | 15 ml (Europe)

Preparation:

1. Mix all the ingredients in a blender until you obtain a smooth smoothie.
2. Serve immediately.

Nutritional information (per serving): Calories: 280 | Proteins: 25 g | Fat: 8 g (Saturated: 1 g) | Carbohydrates: 25 g | Fiber: 5 g | Sugars: 12 g | Sodium: 150 mg

Protein Granola Bars

Preparation time: 15 minutes

Cooking time: 20 minutes

Servings: 4 bars

Ingredients:

- » Oatmeal: 1 cup (USA) | 240 ml (Europe)
- » Protein powder: 2 tbsp (USA) | 60 g (Europe)
- » Walnuts: 1/2 cup (USA) | 120 ml (Europe)
- » Honey: 3 tbsp (USA) | 45 ml (Europe)
- » Dried blueberries: 1/4 cup (USA) | 60 ml (Europe)

Preparation:

1. Mix all the ingredients in a bowl.
2. Spread the mixture in a mold and bake at 350 °F (175 °C) for 20 minutes.
3. Let cool and cut into bars.

Nutritional information (per bar): Calories: 320 | Proteins: 23 g | Fat: 10 g (Saturated: 1.5 g) | Carbohydrates: 38 g | Fiber: 4 g | Sugars: 20 g | Sodium: 60 mg

Tuna and Avocado Rolls

Preparation time: 15 minutes

Cooking time: 0 minutes

Servings: 2 rolls

Ingredients:

» Canned tuna (drained): 1 cup (USA) | 240 ml (Europe)
» Avocado: 1 (USA) | 1 unit (Europe) (chopped)
» Greek yogurt: 2 tbsp (USA) | 30 ml (Europe)
» Whole wheat tortillas: 2 (USA) | 2 units (Europe)
» Lettuce: 1 cup (USA) | 240 ml (Europe)

Preparation:

1. Mix the tuna, avocado, and Greek yogurt in a bowl. Spread on the tortillas, add lettuce, and roll up.

Nutritional information (per roll): Calories: 350 | Proteins: 25 g | Fat: 14 g (Saturated: 2 g) | Carbohydrates: 30 g | Fiber: 5 g | Sugars: 3 g | Sodium: 400 mg

Stuffed Eggs With Chicken

Preparation time: 20 minutes

Cooking time: 10 minutes

Servings: 4 eggs

Ingredients:

» Eggs: 4 (USA) | 4 units (Europe)
» Cooked chicken breast: 3.5 oz (USA) | 100 g (Europe) (crumbled)
» Mustard: 1 tbsp (USA) | 15 ml (Europe)
» Greek yogurt: 2 tbsp (USA) | 30 ml (Europe)

Preparation:

1. Boil the eggs. Cut in half and remove the yolk.
2. Mix the yolk with chicken, mustard, and yogurt.
3. Fill the eggs with the mixture.

Nutritional information (per 2 halves): Calories: 220 | Proteins: 23 g | Fat: 10 g (Saturated: 2 g) | Carbohydrates: 2 g | Fiber: 0 g | Sugars: 1 g | Sodium: 250 mg

Chicken and Black Bean Quesadillas

Preparation time: 15 minutes | **Cooking time:** 10 minutes | **Servings:** 2 quesadillas

Ingredients:

» Whole wheat tortillas: 2 (USA) | 2 units (Europe)
» Cooked chicken breast: 3.5 oz (USA) | 100 g (Europe) (chopped)
» Black beans: 1/2 cup (USA) | 120 ml (Europe)
» Low-fat cheese: 1.7 oz (USA) | 50 g (Europe) (grated)

Preparation:

1. Place the chicken, black beans, and cheese on a tortilla. Cover with another tortilla.
2. Cook in a pan until golden. Flip and cook the other side.

Nutritional information (per quesadilla): Calories: 310 | Proteins: 28 g | Fat: 9 g (Saturated: 4 g) | Carbohydrates: 30 g | Fiber: 5 g | Sugars: 2 g | Sodium: 450 mg

Curry Chicken Bites

Preparation time: 15 minutes

Cooking time: 15 minutes

Servings: 4 bites

Ingredients:

- » Chicken breast: 7 oz (USA) | 200 g (Europe) (cubed)
- » Greek yogurt: 3 tbsp (USA) | 45 ml (Europe)
- » Curry powder: 1 tsp (USA) | 5 ml (Europe)
- » Lemon: 1/2 (USA) | 1/2 unit (Europe) (squeezed)

Preparation:

1. Marinate the chicken with yogurt, curry, and lemon for 30 minutes.
2. Thread onto skewers and cook in a hot pan until golden brown.

Nutritional information (per 2 bites): Calories: 180 | Proteins: 30 g | Fat: 3 g (Saturated: 1 g) | Carbohydrates: 4 g | Fiber: 1 g | Sugars: 2 g | Sodium: 80 mg

Tofu and Pepper Skewers

Preparation time: 20 minutes (plus marinating)

Cooking time: 10 minutes

Servings: 2 skewers

Ingredients:

» Tofu (firm): 7 oz (USA) | 200 g (Europe)
» Peppers: 1 (USA) | 1 unit (Europe) (various colors, in cubes)
» Soy sauce: 2 tbsp (USA) | 30 ml (Europe)
» Sesame oil: 1 tbsp (USA) | 15 ml (Europe)

Preparation:

1. Marinate the tofu in soy sauce and sesame oil for 1 hour.
2. Thread tofu and peppers onto skewers.
3. Cook on a hot grill until golden brown.

Nutritional information (per skewer): Calories: 230 | Proteins: 22 g | Fat: 12 g (Saturated: 2 g) | Carbohydrates: 12 g | Fiber: 3 g | Sugars: 5 g | Sodium: 600 mg

Chickpea and Red Pepper Dip

Preparation time: 10 minutes

Cooking time: 0 minutes

Servings: 4 servings

Ingredients:

» Cooked chickpeas: 1 cup (USA) | 240 ml (Europe)
» Roasted red pepper: 1 (USA) | 1 unit (Europe)
» Olive oil: 2 tbsp (USA) | 30 ml (Europe)
» Tahini: 1 tbsp (USA) | 15 ml (Europe)

Preparation:

1. Blend all ingredients in a blender until smooth.
2. Serve with vegetable sticks or whole wheat bread.

Nutritional information (per serving): Calories: 180 | Proteins: 21 g | Fat: 8 g (Saturated: 1.5 g) | Carbohydrates: 16 g | Fiber: 5 g | Sugars: 3 g | Sodium: 250 mg

Green Protein Smoothie

Preparation time: 5 minutes

Cooking time: 0 minutes

Servings: 2 shakes

Ingredients:

» Spinach: 2 cups (USA) | 480 ml (Europe)
» Protein powder: 2 tbsp (USA) | 60 g (Europe)
» Almond milk: 1 cup (USA) | 240 ml (Europe)
» Chia: 1 tbsp (USA) | 15 ml (Europe)

Preparation:

1. Blend all ingredients in a blender until smooth.
2. Serve immediately.

Nutritional information (per shake): Calories: 220 | Proteins: 30 g | Fat: 6 g (Saturated: 0.5 g) | Carbohydrates: 12 g | Fiber: 4 g | Sugars: 3 g | Sodium: 180 mg

Wrapped Tuna in Lettuce

Preparation time: 10 minutes

Cooking time: 0 minutes

Servings: 4 wrapped

Ingredients:

» Canned tuna (in water): 7 oz (USA) | 200 g (Europe)
» Low-fat mayonnaise: 2 tbsp (USA) | 30 ml (Europe)
» Celery: 1 stalk (USA) | 1 stem (Europe) (chopped)
» Red onion: 1/4 (USA) | 1/4 unit (Europe) (chopped)
» Romaine lettuce: 4 leaves (USA) | 4 sheets (Europe)

Preparation:

1. Mix the drained tuna with mayonnaise, celery, and red onion.
2. Place a portion of the tuna filling on each lettuce leaf and serve.

Nutritional information (per 2 wraps): Calories: 180 | Proteins: 22 g | Fat: 5 g (Saturated: 1 g) | Carbohydrates: 8 g | Fiber: 2 g | Sugars: 3 g | Sodium: 380 mg

Turkey Skewers With Yogurt Sauce

Preparation time: 15 minutes (plus marinating)

Cooking time: 10 minutes

Servings: 4 skewers

Ingredients:

» Turkey breast: 10.6 oz (USA) | 300 g (Europe) (cubed)
» Greek yogurt: 1/2 cup (USA) | 120 ml (Europe)
» Garlic: 2 cloves (chopped)
» Lemon juice: 2 tbsp (USA) | 30 ml (Europe)
» Paprika: 1/2 tsp (USA) | 2.5 ml (Europe)
» Olive oil: 1 tbsp (USA) | 15 ml (Europe)

Preparation:

1. Marinate the turkey in yogurt, garlic, lemon juice, paprika, and olive oil for 1 hour.
2. Thread onto skewers and cook on a hot grill until golden brown.
3. Serve with additional yogurt sauce.

Nutritional information (per 2 skewers): Calories: 260 | Proteins: 30 g | Fat: 7 g (Saturated: 2 g) | Carbohydrates: 15 g | Fiber: 1 g | Sugars: 3 g | Sodium: 270 mg

Egg Rolls With Vegetables and Chicken

Preparation time: 15 minutes

Cooking time: 10 minutes

Servings: 4 rolls

Ingredients:

» Chicken breast: 5.3 oz (USA) | 150 g (Europe) (cut into strips)
» Eggs: 4
» Asparagus: 8 stalks (USA) | 8 stems (Europe) (cut in half)
» Red bell peppers: 1/2 (USA) | 1/2 unit (Europe) (cut into strips)
» Olive oil: 1 tbsp (USA) | 15 ml (Europe)

Preparation:

1. In a frying pan, heat the oil and fry the chicken until well cooked. Set aside.
2. In a bowl, beat the eggs and pour into the pan to form a thin omelet. Cook until firm. Place the chicken, asparagus, and peppers in the center and roll up.
3. Cut into halves and serve.

Nutritional information (per 2 rolls): Calories: 240 | Proteins: 25 g | Fat: 11 g (Saturated: 2 g) | Carbohydrates: 10 g | Fiber: 3 g | Sugars: 5 g | Sodium: 190 mg

Mini Portobello Pizzas With Ricotta Cheese

Preparation time: 10 minutes

Cooking time: 15 minutes

Servings: 4 mini pizzas

Ingredients:

- » Portobello mushrooms: 4 (USA) | 4 units (Europe) (large, stems removed)
- » Ricotta cheese: 1/2 cup (USA) | 120 ml (Europe)
- » Spinach: 1 cup (USA) | 240 ml (Europe) (cut into strips)
- » Chicken breast: 3.5 g (USA) | 100 g (Europe) (cut into strips and cooked)
- » Marinara sauce: 1/2 cup (USA) | 120 ml (Europe)

Preparation:

1. Preheat oven to 375 °F (190 °C).
2. Place the mushrooms on a baking sheet. Add a tablespoon of marinara sauce to each mushroom, followed by the chicken and spinach strips. Top with ricotta cheese.
3. Bake for 15 minutes or until cheese is golden.

Nutritional information (for 2 mini pizzas): Calories: 270 | Protein: 23 g | Fat: 12 g (Saturated: 5 g) | Carbohydrates: 17 g | Fiber: 3 g | Sugars: 6 g | Sodium: 420 mg

Egg White Pancakes

Preparation time: 10 minutes

Cooking time: 5 minutes

Servings: 2

Ingredients:

- » Egg whites: 1 cup (USA) | 240 ml (Europe)
- » Protein powder: 1/4 cup (USA) | 60 ml (Europe) (your choice of flavor)
- » Banana: 1/2 (USA) | 1/2 unit (Europe) (ripe, mashed)
- » Cinnamon: 1/2 teaspoon (USA) | 2.5 ml (Europe)

Preparation:

1. In a bowl, combine all the ingredients until you get a smooth mixture.
2. Heat a nonstick skillet over a medium fire.
3. Pour some of the mixture into the pan to form pancakes.
4. Cook until golden on both sides.
5. Serve hot with your favorite toppings.

Nutritional information (per serving): Calories: 150 | Protein: 28 g | Fat: 1 g (Saturated: ⬚0.1 g) | Carbohydrates: 10 g | Fiber: 2 g | Sugars: 5 g | Sodium: 220 mg.

Chickpea and Tuna Salad

Preparation time: 10 minutes

Cooking time: 0 minutes

Servings: 2

Ingredients:

» Cooked chickpeas: 1 cup (USA) | 240 ml (Europe)
» Canned tuna (plain): 1 can (USA) | 1 can (Europe)
» Tomato: 1 (USA) | 1 unit (Europe) (chopped)
» Red onion: 1/4 (USA) | 60 ml (Europe) (finely chopped)
» Olive oil: 1 tbsp (USA) | 15 ml (Europe)
» Lemon juice: 1 tbsp (USA) | 15 ml (Europe)

Preparation:

1. In a bowl, combine the chickpeas, the drained tuna, the tomato, and the onion.
2. Mix well and dress with olive oil and lemon juice.
3. Serve fresh.

Nutritional information (per serving): Calories: 350 | Protein: 28 g | Fat: 12 g (Saturated: 2 g) | Carbohydrates: 30 g | Fiber: 8 g | Sugars: 6 g | Sodium: 400 mg.

Quinoa With Vegetables and Chicken

Preparation time: 15 minutes

Cooking time: 20 minutes

Servings: 2

Ingredients:

» Quinoa: 1/2 cup (USA) | 120 ml (Europe)
» Chicken breast: 1 (USA) | 1 (Europe) (cut into strips)
» Red bell pepper: 1/2 (USA) | 120 ml (Europe) (cut into strips)
» Asparagus: 6 (USA) | 6 units (Europe)
» Olive oil: 1 tbsp (USA) | 15 ml (Europe)
» Salt and pepper to taste

Preparation:

1. Cook the quinoa following the package instructions.
2. In a pan with olive oil, sauté the chicken until it is golden.
3. Add the bell peppers and asparagus, cooking until just tender.
4. Mix with the cooked quinoa and season with salt and pepper.
5. Serve hot.

Nutritional information (per serving): Calories: 420 | Protein: 30 g | Fat: 14 g (Saturated: ⊠2.5 g) | Carbohydrates: 40 g | Fiber: 6 g | Sugars: 4 g | Sodium: 200 mg.

Tuna and Avocado Wrap

Preparation time: 10 minutes

Cooking time: 0 minutes

Servings: 2

Ingredients:

- » Whole wheat tortillas: 2 (USA) | 2 units (Europe)
- » Canned tuna (plain): 1 can (USA) | 1 can (Europe)
- » Avocado: 1 (USA) | 1 unit (Europe) (cut into slices)
- » Lettuce: 1 cup (USA) | 240 ml (Europe) (chopped)
- » Tomato: 1 (USA) | 1 unit (Europe) (sliced)
- » Mustard: 1 tsp (USA) | 5 ml (Europe)

Preparation:

1. In a bowl, mix the shredded tuna with the mustard.
2. Spread this mixture on each tortilla.
3. Add the avocado, lettuce, and tomato.
4. Roll up and serve.

Nutritional information (per serving): Calories: 320 | Protein: 20 g | Fat: 15 g (Saturated: 2.5 g) | Carbohydrates: 30 g | Fiber: 7 g | Sugars: 4 g | Sodium: 400 mg.

Quinoa With Vegetables and Tofu

Preparation time: 10 minutes

Cooking time: 25 minutes

Servings: 2

Ingredients:

» Quinoa: 1/2 cup (USA) | 120 ml (Europe)
» Firm tofu: 7 oz (USA) | 200 g (Europe) (cut into cubes)
» Broccoli: 1 cup (USA) | 240 ml (Europe) (cut into florets)
» Red bell peppers: 1/2 (USA) | 1/2 unit (Europe) (cut into strips)
» Sesame oil: 2 tbsp (USA) | 30 ml (Europe)
» Soy sauce: 2 tbsp (USA) | 30 ml (Europe)

Preparation:

1. Cook quinoa according to package instructions.
2. Meanwhile, sauté tofu in sesame oil until golden brown.
3. Add the broccoli and peppers and cook until tender.
4. Mix with the quinoa and add the soy sauce.

Nutritional information (per serving): Calories: 420 | Protein: 24 g | Fat: 14 g (Saturated: 2 g) | Carbohydrates: 52 g | Fiber: 10g | Sugars: 6 g | Sodium: 630 mg

Rice and Egg Bowl With Spinach

Preparation time: 10 minutes

Cooking time: 20 minutes

Servings: 2

Ingredients:

- » Brown rice: 1 cup (USA) | 240 ml (Europe) (cooked)
- » Eggs: 4 (USA) | 4 units (Europe)
- » Fresh spinach: 2 cups (USA) | 480 ml (Europe)
- » Cherry tomatoes: 1/2 cup (USA) | 120 ml (Europe) (cut in half)
- » Olive oil: 1 tbsp (USA) | 15 ml (Europe)
- » Pepper and salt to taste

Preparation:

1. In a frying pan, heat the olive oil and fry the eggs. Add spinach until tender.
2. Serve the eggs and spinach over the cooked brown rice and add the cherry tomatoes.
3. Season with salt and pepper.

Nutritional information (per serving): Calories: 380 | Protein: 22 g | Fat: 16 g (Saturated: 4 g) | Carbohydrates: 40 g | Fiber: 6g | Sugars: 3 g | Sodium: 150 mg

Blackberry and Chia Smoothie

Preparation time: 5 minutes

Cooking time: 0 minutes

Servings: 2

Ingredients:

» Blackberries: 1 cup (USA) | 240 ml (Europe)
» Almond milk: 2 cups (USA) | 480 ml (Europe)
» Chia seeds: 2 tbsp (USA) | 30 ml (Europe)
» Protein powder: 2 tbsp (USA) | 60 g (Europe)
» Honey: 1 tbsp (USA) | 15 ml (Europe)

Preparation:

1. Blend all ingredients in a blender until smooth. Serve immediately.

Nutritional information (per serving): Calories: 320 | Protein: 24 g | Fat: 10 g (Saturated: 1 g) | Carbohydrates: 38g | Fiber: 12g | Sugars: 20 g | Sodium: 190 mg

Chicken Breast With Almond Sauce

Preparation time: 10 minutes

Cooking time: 15 minutes

Servings: 2

Ingredients:

» Chicken breasts: 2 (USA) | 2 units (Europe)
» Almonds: 1/3 cup (USA) | 80 ml (Europe) (ground)
» Garlic: 2 cloves
» Chicken broth: 1/2 cup (USA) | 120 ml (Europe)
» Olive oil: 1 tbsp (USA) | 15 ml (Europe)
» Salt and pepper to taste

Preparation:

1. Sauté chicken breasts in olive oil until golden brown. Remove and reserve.
2. In the same pan, add the garlic and ground almonds. Add the broth and simmer until thickened.
3. Serve the breasts and cover with the sauce.

Nutritional information (per serving): Calories: 340 | Protein: 32 g | Fat: 18 g (Saturated: 2 g) | Carbohydrates: 10 g | Fiber: 3 g | Sugars: 2 g | Sodium: 220 mg

Mushroom and Asparagus Omelet

Preparation time: 10 minutes

Cooking time: 10 minutes

Servings: 2

Ingredients:

» Eggs: 4 (USA) | 4 units (Europe)
» Mushrooms: 1 cup (USA) | 240 ml (Europe) (sliced)
» Asparagus: 1 cup (USA) | 240 ml (Europe) (chopped)
» Feta cheese: 1/2 cup (USA) | 120 ml (Europe)
» Olive oil: 1 tbsp (USA) | 15 ml (Europe)
» Salt and pepper to taste

Preparation:

1. Sauté mushrooms and asparagus in oil until tender.
2. Beat the eggs and add to the pan. Cook until set and add the feta cheese on top.
3. Serve hot.

Nutritional information (per serving): Calories: 320 | Protein: 22 g | Fat: 22 g (Saturated: 8 g) | Carbohydrates: 10 g | Fiber: 3 g | Sugars: 5 g | Sodium: 420 mg

Turkey and Hummus Wraps

Preparation time: 10 minutes

Cooking time: 0 minutes

Servings: 2

Ingredients:

- » Whole wheat tortillas: 2 (USA) | 2 units (Europe)
- » Cooked turkey: 6 oz (USA) | 170 g (Europe) (sliced)
- » Hummus: 1/2 cup (USA) | 120 ml (Europe)
- » Lettuce: 1 cup (USA) | 240 ml (Europe) (chopped)
- » Tomato: 1 (USA) | 1 unit (Europe) (sliced)
- » Cucumber: 1/2 (USA) | 1/2 unit (Europe) (sliced)

Preparation:

1. Spread the hummus on each tortilla.
2. Add the turkey slices, lettuce, tomato, and cucumber.
3. Roll up and serve.

Nutritional information (per serving): Calories: 400 | Protein: 28 g | Fat: 12 g (Saturated: 2 g) | Carbohydrates: 48 g | Fiber: 7 g | Sugars: 4 g | Sodium: 670 mg

Lentil and Chorizo Soup

Preparation time: 15 minutes

Cooking time: 40 minutes

Servings: 2

Ingredients:

» Lentils: 1 cup (USA) | 240 ml (Europe) (soaked)
» Chorizo: 4 oz (USA) | 115 g (Europe) (chopped)
» Onion: 1 (USA) | 1 unit (Europe) (chopped)
» Garlic: 2 cloves (chopped)
» Chicken broth: 4 cups (USA) | 960 ml (Europe)
» Olive oil: 1 tbsp (USA) | 15 ml (Europe)
» Salt and pepper to taste

Preparation:

1. In a pot, sauté the chorizo, onion, and garlic in olive oil.
2. Add the lentils and broth. Cook until the lentils are tender.
3. Season with salt and pepper.

Nutritional information (per serving): Calories: 440 | Protein: 28 g | Fat: 18 g (Saturated: 6 g) | Carbohydrates: 40 g | Fiber: 16 g | Sugars: 4 g | Sodium: 750 mg

Chocolate and Peanut Butter Smoothie

Preparation time: 5 minutes

Cooking time: 0 minutes

Servings: 2

Ingredients:

- » Almond milk: 2 cups (USA) | 480 ml (Europe)
- » Cocoa powder: 2 tbsp (USA) | 30 ml (Europe)
- » Peanut butter: 2 tbsp (USA) | 30 ml (Europe)
- » Protein powder: 2 tbsp (USA) | 60 g (Europe)
- » Banana: 1 (USA) | 1 unit (Europe)

Preparation:

1. Blend all ingredients in a blender until smooth. Serve immediately.

Nutritional information (per serving): Calories: 400 | Proteins: 30 g | Fat: 16 g (Saturated: 3.5 g) | Carbohydrates: 35 g | Fiber: 7 g | Sugars: 16 g | Sodium: 200 mg

Smoked Salmon Toasts

Preparation time: 10 minutes

Cooking time: 2 minutes

Servings: 2

Ingredients:

» Whole wheat bread: 4 slices
» Smoked salmon: 4 oz (USA) | 115 g (Europe)
» Light cream cheese: 1/2 cup (USA) | 120 ml (Europe)
» Chives: 2 tbsp (USA) | 30 ml (Europe) (chopped)
» Lemon: 1 (USA) | 1 unit (Europe) (squeezed)
» Salt and pepper to taste

Preparation:

1. Toast the bread.
2. Spread the cream cheese over each slice.
3. Place the smoked salmon on top, add the chives, and a few drops of lemon, and season with salt and pepper.

Nutritional information (per serving): Calories: 360 | Protein: 24 g | Fat: 12 g (Saturated: 4 g) | Carbohydrates: 36 g | Fiber: 5 g | Sugars: 4 g | Sodium: 650 mg

Chicken and Avocado Wraps

Preparation time: 15 minutes

Cooking time: 10 minutes

Servings: 2

Ingredients:

- » Whole wheat tortillas: 2 (USA) | 2 units (Europe)
- » Chicken breast: 6 oz (USA) | 170 g (Europe) (chopped)
- » Avocado: 1 (USA) | 1 unit (Europe) (sliced)
- » Tomato: 1 (USA) | 1 unit (Europe) (sliced)
- » Lettuce: 1 cup (USA) | 240 ml (Europe) (chopped)
- » Yogurt sauce: 1/4 cup (USA) | 60 ml (Europe)
- » Olive oil: 1 tbsp (USA) | 15 ml (Europe)
- » Salt and pepper to taste

Preparation:

1. Sauté chicken in olive oil until golden brown.
2. In each tortilla, place the chicken, avocado, tomato, lettuce, and yogurt sauce.
3. Roll up and serve.

Nutritional information (per serving):

Calories: 420 | Protein: 32 g | Fat: 20 g (Saturated: 3.5 g) | Carbohydrates: 35 g | Fiber: 10 g | Sugars: 5 g | Sodium: 450 mg

Recovery: Post-Workout Meals

Banana Protein Shake

Preparation time: 5 minutes

Cooking time: 0 minutes

Servings: 2

Ingredients:

- » Almond milk: 2 cups (USA) | 480 ml (Europe)
- » Banana: 1 (USA) | 1 unit (Europe)
- » Protein powder: 2 scoops (USA) | 30 ml (Europe)
- » Honey: 1 tsp (USA) | 5 ml (Europe)
- » Cocoa powder: 1 tsp (USA) | 5 ml (Europe)

Preparation:

1. In a blender, combine all the ingredients.
2. Mix until you get a smooth consistency.
3. Serve immediately in glasses.

Nutritional information (per serving): Calories: 280 | Protein: 24 g | Fat: 5 g (Saturated: 1 g) | Carbohydrates: 40 g | Fiber: 4 g | Sugars: 20 g | Sodium: 90 mg.

Chicken Breast With Quinoa and Vegetables

Preparation time: 10 minutes

Cooking time: 20 minutes

Servings: 2

Ingredients:

» Chicken breasts: 2 (USA) | 2 (Europe)
» Quinoa: 1 cup (USA) | 240 ml (Europe)
» Water: 2 cups (USA) | 480 ml (Europe)
» Broccoli: 1 cup (USA) | 240 ml (Europe) (cut into florets)
» Carrot: 1 (USA) | 1 unit (Europe) (chopped)
» Olive oil: 2 tsp (USA) | 10 ml (Europe)
» Salt and pepper to taste

Preparation:

1. In a skillet, heat 1 tsp of olive oil and cook the chicken breasts until golden brown or until your desired doneness. Set aside.
2. In a saucepan, bring the water to a boil and add the quinoa, cooking according to package directions.
3. In a separate skillet, heat 1 tsp of olive oil and sauté the broccoli and carrot until tender.
4. Mix the quinoa with the vegetables and serve along with the chicken.

Nutritional information (per serving): Calories: 380 | Protein: 30 g | Fat: 9 g (Saturated: 1.5 g) | Carbohydrates: 45 g | Fiber: 6 g | Sugars: 3 g | Sodium: 220 mg.

Quinoa With Chicken and Broccoli

Preparation time: 10 minutes

Cooking time: 20 minutes

Servings: 2

Ingredients:

» Quinoa: 1 cup (US) | 240 ml (Europe)
» Chicken breast: 6 oz (US) | 170 g (Europe) (chopped)
» Broccoli: 1 cup (US) | 240 ml (Europe) (chopped)
» Garlic: 2 cloves (chopped)
» Chicken broth: 2 cups (US) | 480 ml (Europe)
» Olive oil: 2 tbsp (US) | 30 ml (Europe)
» Salt and pepper to taste

Preparation:

1. Cook the quinoa in the broth until tender.
2. Meanwhile, sauté the chicken and garlic in olive oil.
3. Add the broccoli and cook until tender.
4. Mix with the cooked quinoa and serve.

Nutritional information (per serving): Calories: 460 | Proteins: 30 g | Fat: 14 g (Saturated: 2 g) | Carbohydrates: 50 g | Fiber: 6 g | Sugars: 3 g | Sodium: 500 mg

Tuna and Chickpea Salad

Preparation time: 10 minutes

Cooking time: 0 minutes

Servings: 2

Ingredients:

» Canned tuna (in water): 1 can (USA) | 1 can (Europe)
» Cooked chickpeas: 1 cup (USA) | 240 ml (Europe)
» Cucumber: 1 (USA) | 1 unit (Europe) (chopped)
» Cherry tomatoes: 1/2 cup (USA) | 120 ml (Europe) (halved)
» Olive oil: 1 tbsp (USA) | 15 ml (Europe)
» Lemon juice: 1 tbsp (USA) | 15 ml (Europe)
» Salt and pepper to taste

Preparation:

1. Mix the tuna, chickpeas, cucumber, and tomatoes in a bowl.
2. Combine the olive oil, lemon juice, salt, and pepper in a small bowl and pour over the salad. Mix well.
3. Serve immediately.

Nutritional information (per serving): Calories: 320 | Protein: 28 g | Fat: 12 g (Saturated: 2 g) | Carbohydrates: 30 g | Fiber: 7 g | Sugars: 6 g | Sodium: 400 mg.

Blueberry and Spinach Smoothie

Preparation time: 5 minutes

Cooking time: 0 minutes

Servings: 2

Ingredients:

» Almond milk: 2 cups (USA) | 480 ml (Europe)
» Fresh spinach: 1 cup (USA) | 240 ml (Europe)
» Blueberries: 1/2 cup (USA) | 120 ml (Europe)
» Protein powder: 2 scoops (USA) | 30 ml (Europe)
» Chia seeds: 1 tsp (USA) | 5 ml (Europe)

Preparation:

1. Combine all the ingredients in a blender.
2. Mix until smooth.
3. Serve immediately.

Nutritional information (per serving): Calories: 250 | Protein: 25 g | Fat: 6 g (Saturated: 0.5 g) | Carbohydrates: 30 g | Fiber: 5 g | Sugars: 18 g | Sodium: 150 mg.

Rice With Chicken and Vegetables

Preparation time: 15 minutes

Cooking time: 25 minutes

Servings: 2

Ingredients:

» Chicken breast: 2 (USA) | 2 (Europe) (cut into strips)
» Brown rice: 1 cup (USA) | 240 ml (Europe)
» Broccoli: 1 cup (USA) | 240 ml (Europe) (cut into florets)
» Red bell pepper: 1 (USA) | 1 unit (Europe) (cut into strips)
» Soy sauce: 2 tsp (USA) | 10 ml (Europe)
» Olive oil: 1 tbsp (USA) | 15 ml (Europe)

Preparation:

1. Cook the rice according to the package instructions.
2. In a large skillet, heat the olive oil and fry the chicken until cooked through. Add the vegetables and fry until tender.
3. Add the soy sauce and cooked rice. Stir well.
4. Serve hot.

Nutritional information (per serving): Calories: 400 | Protein: 28 g | Fat: 10 g (Saturated: 2 g) | Carbohydrates: 55 g | Fiber: 6 g | Sugars: 3 g | Sodium: 350 mg.

Turkey and Quinoa Salad

Preparation time: 15 minutes

Cooking time: 15 minutes

Servings: 2

Ingredients:

- » Roast turkey (skinless): 1 cup (USA) | 240 ml (Europe) (diced)
- » Quinoa: 1/2 cup (USA) | 120 ml (Europe)
- » Cherry tomatoes: 1/2 cup (USA) | 120 ml (Europe) (halved)
- » Cucumber: 1/2 (USA) | 1/2 unit (Europe) (chopped)
- » Olive oil: 1 tbsp (USA) | 15 ml (Europe)
- » Lemon juice: 1 tbsp (USA) | 15 ml (Europe)
- » Salt and pepper to taste

Preparation:

1. Cook the quinoa according to the package instructions.
2. In a large bowl, combine the turkey, quinoa, tomatoes, and cucumber.
3. Combine olive oil, lemon juice, salt, and pepper in a small bowl. Pour over the salad and mix well.
4. Serve cold or at room temperature.

Nutritional information (per serving): Calories: 360 | Protein: 30 g | Fat: 12 g (Saturated: 2 g) | Carbohydrates: 35 g | Fiber: 5 g | Sugars: 4 g | Sodium: 250 mg.

Lentil and Tuna Salad

Preparation time: 10 minutes

Cooking time: 20 minutes (if the lentils are not previously cooked)

Servings: 2

Ingredients:

» Cooked lentils: 1 cup (USA) | 240 ml (Europe)
» Canned tuna (in water): 1 can (USA) | 1 can (Europe)
» Red onion: 1/4 (USA) | 1/4 unit (Europe) (finely chopped)
» Cherry tomatoes: 1/2 cup (USA) | 120 ml (Europe) (halved)
» Olive oil: 1 tbsp (USA) | 15 ml (Europe)
» Balsamic vinegar: 1 tbsp (USA) | 15 ml (Europe)
» Salt and pepper to taste

Preparation:

1. In a large bowl, combine the lentils, tuna, onion, and tomatoes.
2. In a small bowl, combine the olive oil, balsamic vinegar, salt, and pepper. Pour over the salad and mix well.
3. Serve cold or at room temperature.

Nutritional information (per serving): Calories: 310 | Protein: 28 g | Fat: 8 g (Saturated: 1 g) | Carbohydrates: 35 g | Fiber: 10 g | Sugars: 4 g | Sodium: 320 mg.

Whole Grain Pasta With Chicken and Broccoli

Preparation time: 15 minutes

Cooking time: 20 minutes

Servings: 2

Ingredients:

» Whole wheat pasta: 2 cups (USA) | 480 ml (Europe) (uncooked)
» Chicken breasts: 2 (USA) | 2 (Europe) (cut into strips)
» Broccoli: 1 cup (USA) | 240 ml (Europe) (cut into florets)
» Garlic: 2 cloves (USA) | 2 cloves (Europe) (minced)
» Olive oil: 1 tbsp (USA) | 15 ml (Europe)
» Salt and pepper to taste

Preparation:

1. Cook the pasta according to the package instructions.
2. In a skillet, heat the olive oil and fry the garlic. Add the chicken and cook until golden brown or until your desired doneness.
3. Add the broccoli and sauté until tender but still crisp.
4. Mix the cooked pasta with the chicken and broccoli.
5. Serve hot with a drizzle of olive oil, salt, and pepper to taste.

Nutritional information (per serving): Calories: 420 | Protein: 32 g | Fat: 10 g (Saturated: 2 g) | Carbohydrates: 55 g | Fiber: 8 g | Sugars: 4 g | Sodium: 180 mg.

Whole Grain Pasta With Tuna

Preparation time: 10 minutes

Cooking time: 15 minutes

Servings: 2

Ingredients:

» Whole wheat pasta: 2 cups (US) | 480 ml (Europe)
» Natural tuna: 1 can (US) | 150 g (Europe)
» Cherry tomatoes: 1 cup (US) | 240 ml (Europe) (halved)
» Olive oil: 2 tbsp (US) | 30 ml (Europe)
» Garlic: 2 cloves (chopped)
» Basil: 1/4 cup (US) | 60 ml (Europe) (chopped)
» Salt and pepper to taste

Preparation:

1. Cook pasta according to package instructions.
2. Meanwhile, in a skillet, sauté garlic in olive oil. Add the tuna and tomatoes. Cook until tender.
3. Mix with the pasta, add the basil, salt, and pepper.

Nutritional Information (per serving): Calories: 480 | Protein: 28 g | Fat: 15 g (Saturated: 2.5 g) | Carbohydrates: 60 g | Fiber: 8 g | Sugars: 5 g | Sodium: 370 mg

Turkey Rolls With Hummus and Peppers

Preparation time: 10 minutes

Cooking time: 0 minutes

Servings: 2

Ingredients:

- » Sliced turkey breast: 6 slices (USA) | 6 slices (Europe)
- » Hummus: 1/4 cup (USA) | 60 ml (Europe)
- » Roasted red peppers: 1/2 cup (USA) | 120 ml (Europe) (striped)

Preparation:

1. Spread a tablespoon of hummus over each slice of turkey.
2. Place a few strips of roasted red pepper in the center of each slice.
3. Roll the turkey slices around the peppers.
4. Serve immediately.

Nutritional information (per serving): Calories: 160 | Protein: 22 g | Fat: 4 g (Saturated: 1 g) | Carbohydrates: 9 g | Fiber: 3 g | Sugars: 3 g | Sodium: 780 mg.

Brown Rice With Shrimp and Peas

Preparation time: 10 minutes

Cooking time: 20 minutes

Servings: 2

Ingredients:

- » Brown rice: 1 cup (USA) | 240 ml (Europe) (cooked)
- » Shrimp: 1/2 lb (USA) | 225 g (Europe) (peeled and deveined)
- » Peas: 1/2 cup (USA) | 120 ml (Europe)
- » Garlic: 2 cloves (USA) | 2 cloves (Europe) (minced)
- » Olive oil: 1 tbsp (USA) | 15 ml (Europe)
- » Salt and pepper to taste

Preparation:

1. Heat the olive oil in a skillet over a medium-high fire.
2. Add the garlic and fry until fragrant.
3. Add the shrimp and cook until they are pink.
4. Add the peas and cook until tender.
5. Add the cooked rice and mix well.
6. Season with salt and pepper to taste.
7. Serve hot.

Nutritional information (per serving): Calories: 330 | Protein: 25 g | Fat: 7 g (Saturated: 1 g) | Carbohydrates: 42 g | Fiber: 3 g | Sugars: 2 g | Sodium: 330 mg.

Tuna Salad With Chickpeas

Preparation time: 15 minutes

Cooking time: 0 minutes

Servings: 2

Ingredients:

» Canned tuna (plain): 1 can (USA) | 1 can (Europe) (drained)
» Cooked chickpeas: 1 cup (USA) | 240 ml (Europe)
» Cherry tomatoes: 1/2 cup (USA) | 120 ml (Europe) (halved)
» Cucumber: 1/2 (USA) | 1/2 (Europe) (cut into thin slices)
» Red onion: 1/4 (USA) | 1/4 unit (Europe) (finely chopped)
» Extra virgin olive oil: 2 tbsp (USA) | 30 ml (Europe)
» Lemon juice: 1 tbsp (USA) | 15 ml (Europe)
» Salt and pepper to taste
» Fresh parsley: 2 tbsp (USA) | 30 ml (Europe) (finely chopped)

Preparation:

1. In a large bowl, combine the tuna, chickpeas, cherry tomatoes, cucumber, and red onion.
2. In a separate bowl, mix the olive oil, lemon juice, salt, and pepper.
3. Pour the dressing over the salad and toss well so that everything is well combined.
4. Garnish with the chopped fresh parsley.
5. Serve immediately.

Nutritional information (per serving): Calories: 360 | Protein: 25 g | Fat: 14 g (Saturated: 2 g) | Carbohydrates: 35 g | Fiber: 9 g | Sugars: 6 g | Sodium: 320 mg.

Throughout this chapter, you've been equipped with an arsenal of recipes designed specifically to nourish, energize, and restore the body you work so hard to sculpt. Each ingredient, each combination, and each dish has been selected with your bodybuilding goals in mind. You now have the culinary tools to maximize every workout, ensuring your diet supports your efforts in the gym.

But, as you well know, bodybuilding and physical transformation do not end in the kitchen or the gym. It's a holistic lifestyle that encompasses multiple aspects, from sleep and recovery to mindset and motivation. Each element is interconnected, and while nutrition is one piece of the puzzle, there are many more dimensions to explore.

I encourage you not to stop here. Keep moving forward, keep learning. We'll explore another facet of bodybuilding in the following chapter, offering you additional resources and information to keep getting better. You are displaying commitment to your objectives and well-being if you have made a commitment to the recipes in this chapter. Don't let that inclination go.

Chapter 5

Tips From Champions — Bodybuilders and Their Meal Prep Strategies

You come to understand that the gym is merely one component of your overall physical transformation as you move along in the process. The saying "abs are made in the kitchen" may sound corny, but it is unquestionably true.

How do top bodybuilders control their diets? How can you ensure that every calorie, every gram of protein, and every drop of water are utilized to their fullest potential? How can you strike a balance between a prep diet's rigor and your need for energy and recovery?

We shall explore the realm of champions in this chapter and learn their secrets.

Before getting into the exact tactics, it's important to comprehend the theory behind bodybuilder diet preparation. It involves considerably more than merely tracking protein or calorie intake. It's a methodical, even scientific procedure that mixes a chef's dexterity with the biochemistry of the human body.

Ensuring the body receives the nutrients it requires at the right time is the primary goal of meal preparation. To maintain proper muscle definition and control the proportion of body fat, a balance must be struck between the nourishment needed to recover from and grow after intensive exercises.

Champion bodybuilders frequently employ the "batch cook" method. In other words, they plan all of their meals for the following several days on a single day of the week, usually Sunday. The temptation to stray from the diet is removed, saving time during the week. When you have your meals ready and on hand, you're less likely to be tempted.

But batch cooking doesn't mean simply roasting chicken and boiling rice in large quantities. It requires precise planning. The amount of protein, carbohydrate, and fat is calculated based on the individual's daily needs. Meals are designed with the type of training of the day in mind. Intense training days might call for more carbohydrates, while rest or recovery days might focus more on protein and healthy fats.

To talk about food preparation in bodybuilding, supplements should be mentioned. While whole, natural foods are the foundation of any bodybuilding diet, supplements provide that extra bit needed in certain circumstances. For example, immediately after a workout, the body needs a quick dose of protein. This is where a protein shake is more beneficial than a chicken fillet.

Don't rely solely on supplements. They should complement the diet, not replace it. Champions understand this and use supplements strategically to maximize their benefits while maintaining a solid and balanced diet.

Despite all the planning and science behind food preparation, remember that each body is unique. What works for one champion might not work for another. Therefore, you must learn to listen to your body and adjust your diet according to your needs.

Some bodybuilders need more carbohydrates to sustain their energy, while others may require more fat. Signs such as constant fatigue, lack of progress in the gym, or difficulty recovering indicate a need to adjust your diet.

Bodybuilding success is a personal journey, but with the appropriate equipment and the correct attitude, you may achieve heights you never thought possible. Prepare to delve into the champions' secrets right now.

Master Class: Secrets of Professional Bodybuilding Athletes

A thorough knowledge of human physiology and nutrition is combined with discipline, commitment, and passion in the sport of professional bodybuilding. Success in this sport requires both physical prowess and a sound dietary plan. In this section, I'll expose you to some of the best-kept secrets and methods used by competitive bodybuilders to improve both their performance and appearance:

Individualized Nutritional Planning

Individualized nutritional planning is one of the fundamental pillars to achieve success in body-building and, in general, in any health or fitness goal.

While general guidelines are helpful, there is no "one size fits all" when it comes to nutrition. Each person is unique, with different needs, goals, metabolisms, and preferences. Here I will guide you through the process of designing your individualized nutrition plan:

#1: Set Your Goals

Before diving into the nutritional details, you need to clearly define your goals. Are you looking to gain muscle mass, reduce fat, maintain your current weight, or perhaps a combination of these? Your goal will influence your nutritional decisions, from total calorie count to macronutrient ratio.

#2: Calculate Your Caloric Needs

Your daily caloric intake should be consistent with your goals. To determine your needs:

- Maintenance: Start by calculating your Basal Metabolic Rate (BMR), which is the number of calories your body needs at rest. Then multiply that number by an activity factor (sedentary, light, moderate, very active) to get your maintenance calories.

- *Muscle gain:* Add 10–20% to your maintenance calories.
- *Fat loss:* Reduce your maintenance calories by 10–20%.

Many online calculators help with this, but it's important to remember that these numbers are only initial estimates.

#3: Determine Your Macronutrients

Once you have your caloric needs, it's time to break them down into macronutrients: protein, carbohydrates, and fat.

- Proteins: For bodybuilding, between 1.6 and 2.2 grams of protein per kilogram of body weight is recommended. This amount ensures recovery and muscle growth.

- *Carbohydrates:* They fill your glycogen stores, giving you energy to train intensely. The amount needed varies by individual, but a general recommendation might be between 3 and 6 grams per kilogram of body weight.
- *Fats:* Fats are needed for hormonal functions and general health. Once you've allocated calories to protein and carbohydrates, the rest comes from fat. Generally, this translates to around 20–30% of your daily calories.

#4: Consider Your Micronutrients

In addition to macronutrients, make sure you're getting enough vitamins and minerals. These support general health and influence recovery and performance. Include a variety of foods in your diet: fruits, vegetables, whole grains, lean meats, and sources of healthy fats to cover your bases.

#5: Plan Your Meals

With your macronutrient and calorie structure in hand, it's time to start planning your meals. Some people prefer to have 3 large meals and a few snacks. Others opt for 5–6 smaller meals throughout the day. There is no "correct" approach; it's more a matter of personal preference and how your body feels.

It is vital to keep in mind your training schedule. For instance, you might want to have a protein-rich meal after your workout to enhance recuperation, followed by a meal high in carbohydrates before your session to optimize energy.

#6: Monitor and Adjust

Evaluate your success after adhering to your strategy for a few weeks. Are you achieving your objectives? If not, you might need to change your strategy. This could refer to the overall number of calories, the balance of macronutrients, or even the standard of your meal.

#7: Consider Personal Preferences and Sensitivities

Some people just have different eating choices, such as being vegetarian or vegan, or they have food intolerances or allergies. When making plans, they must be considered. Fortunately, there are solutions for practically every need given the broad range of meals readily available nowadays.

Bodybuilders and elite athletes have begun to embrace the sophisticated dietary approach known as carbohydrate cycling. To increase fat burning and muscular function while reducing fat accumulation, the aim is to alternate days of high, moderate, and low carb intake. We examine carb cycling in more detail below, along with its advantages for your training and performance.

Carbohydrate Cycling

Alternating between periods of high and low carbohydrate consumption is known as carbohydrate cycling. Days with high consumption often involve hard workouts, whilst days with low consumption usually involve rest or little exercise. The idea is to combine the benefits of a high-carb diet's performance and energy with a low-carb diet's ability to burn fat.

Consuming carbs before and after strenuous exercise enhances recovery and performance by replacing muscle glycogen reserves, among other advantages.

Days, low in carbohydrates, make the body more effective at burning fat for energy, promoting weight reduction.

Instead of strictly adhering to a high or low-carb diet, cycling offers some variability, making it easier to stick with in the long run.

Implementation of Carbohydrate Cycling

Follow these recommendations:

High Carb Days

These days are intended to replenish your glycogen stores. The exact amount of carbohydrates will vary by individual, but a commonly quoted figure is between 2 and 2.5 grams of carbohydrates per kilogram of body weight. These days are ideal for when you do heavy or high-volume workouts.

Moderate Carb Days

These days range from 1 to 1.5 grams per kilogram of body weight. One option is to align them with moderate-intensity workouts or active recovery days.

Low Carb Days

Here, the intake could be 0.5 grams per kilogram of body weight or even less. These days are better for complete rest or light training.

You must keep the following tips in mind:

- If you are constantly fatigued or don't see the expected results, you will need to adjust the numbers.
- Prioritize complex carbohydrates from sources like sweet potatoes, oats, fruits, and whole grains. However, post-workout, some athletes opt for fast-digesting carbohydrates, such as maltodextrin protein shakes, for quick replenishment.
- Even if you're focusing on carbohydrates, don't neglect adequate protein and fat intake. Protein is crucial for muscle growth and repair, while fats support hormonal and cellular functions.

With changes in carbohydrate intake, the water levels in the body fluctuate. Be sure to drink enough water to stay hydrated.

Smart Supplementation

Stores and websites are full of powders, pills, and tonics, each promising to be the key to bodybuilding success. The secret is not in how many supplements you take, but in how and when you use them. "Smart Supplementation" is the art of choosing and using supplements based on science, individual needs, and specific goals. Here is an in-depth guide on how to apply this strategy on your path to the ideal physique:

Why Supplement?

Proper nutrition is essential for any bodybuilder, and while most nutritional needs must be met through whole foods, supplements are useful tools. They fill nutritional gaps, improve performance, speed recovery, and aid in muscle building. The key is knowing which ones are effective and how to use them properly.

Fundamental Supplements

These are the supplements you should have:

Protein Powder

Promotes muscle repair and growth. Popular sources include whey, casein, and plant-based options like pea protein.

Creatine

One of the most researched supplements, creatine enhances ATP production, which increases performance in high-intensity exercise and promotes muscle growth.

Beta-Alanine

It helps in the production of carnosine, a dipeptide that fights the accumulation of acid in the muscles during intense exercise, improving performance and resistance.

BCAAs (Branched Chain Amino Acids)

These amino acids (leucine, isoleucine, valine) support muscle recovery and reduce fatigue during training.

Omega 3

These fats have anti-inflammatory properties that influence recovery.

Vitamins and Minerals

Particularly those that athletes may need in greater amounts, such as magnesium, zinc, and vitamin D, among others.

Specific Supplements According to Objectives

Now I will give you a guide to use supplements according to the objectives that you may have set yourself:

For Muscle Gain

In addition to protein, consider HMB (leucine metabolite) or supplements that increase nitric oxide production to improve blood flow to the muscle.

For Fat Loss

L-carnitine, CLA (conjugated linoleic acid), and thermogenic like caffeine and green tea extract are helpful, although it's always crucial to do your research and consult with a professional.

Finally, here are some recommendations:

- Supplements are supplements, not replacements. Make sure your diet is solid and balanced before introducing supplements.
- Not all supplements are the same. Look for products backed by scientific research and avoid falling into marketing traps.
- It is better to have a few high-quality supplements than an arsenal of products of questionable efficacy.

At some periods, some vitamins are more effective. For instance, whereas casein digests slowly and is better before bed, whey protein is fast absorbed and great post-workout.

Always work with a sports nutritionist or physician before using supplements, particularly if you use medication or have a particular medical condition.

Chrono-nutrition

Many people may not be aware of the phrase chrono-nutrition, yet every professional bodybuilder and anybody trying to maximize growth and recovery must understand its idea. This field integrates nutrition with the study of chronobiology, which investigates how our biological clock controls some physiological functions. You may increase your outcomes and enhance your general health by timing your food intake with your body's natural cycles.

It is predicated on the notion that when we eat matters just as much as what we consume. Every person has an inbuilt circadian clock that controls a number of functions, including metabolism and sleep. This clock is influenced by food, and our clock governs how we metabolize food.

Benefits of Chrono-nutrition

These benefits will motivate you to implement it:

Metabolism Optimization

Eating in tune with our biological clock increases metabolic efficiency, which means better digestion and nutrient absorption.

Improvement in Body Composition

Chrono-nutrition reduces body fat and promotes muscle gain by aligning the intake of nutrients with the times when the body uses them most efficiently.

Increased Energy and Recovery

Eating at the right times ensures that you have energy when you need it and that your body recovers quickly after exercise.

How to Put Chrono-nutrition Into Practice

Follow these recommendations:

Breakfast

Your body has been fasting overnight. Breakfast restarts your metabolism. It includes protein, healthy fats, and complex carbohydrates to ensure an energetic start to the day. Avoid refined sugars that cause spikes and dips in energy levels.

Lunch

This should be your largest meal if you follow a traditional chrono-nutrition pattern. Your metabolism is at its highest at noon, and it processes food more efficiently.

Dinner

Ideally, dinner should be lighter and eaten at least 2–3 hours before bed. This allows for proper digestion before your body goes into recovery mode during sleep.

Avoid Eating Right Before Bed

The body slows down its metabolic activity during sleep, so food eaten just before sleep is more easily stored as fat.

Respect Feeding Windows

If you practice intermittent fasting, combine it with chrono-nutrition. For example, if you eat in an 8-hour window, make sure that window aligns with your circadian rhythm.

Pre-Workout

Make sure you have a meal rich in complex carbohydrates and protein about 1–2 hours before your workout.

Post-Workout

After training, your anabolic window is open. Consume protein and carbohydrates to make the most of this opportunity for recovery and growth.

While chrono-nutrition offers guidelines, each individual is unique. Pay attention to how you feel. If you're hungry at night or feel low on energy during the day, adjust your schedule. The key is to find a balance that works for you and aligns with your bodybuilding goals.

Nutritional Periodization

Nutritional periodization is an advanced strategy that tailors nutrition to meet the specific needs of different phases of training. This technique allows athletes, especially bodybuilders, to maximize their performance, recovery, and long-term adaptations.

Like periodization of training, where programs are divided into specific phases to address different goals, nutritional periodization considers the athlete's entire cycle to deliver the right input at the right time.

Fundamentals of Nutritional Periodization

The main purpose of nutritional periodization is to align food and nutrient intake with the energy and metabolic requirements of the different phases of training. Through this alignment, it seeks to:

- Optimize performance during training sessions.
- Improve post-training recovery.
- Facilitate specific accommodations that the training program tries to achieve.
- Manage body composition, such as gaining muscle mass and/or losing fat.

Basic Structure

Nutritional periodization is based on phases or cycles, which vary in duration, but are generally divided into:

- Loading phase: Focuses on increasing muscle mass. It requires a caloric surplus and higher protein and carbohydrate intake.

- Definition phase: Aims to reduce fat while maintaining muscle mass. It implies a caloric deficit and adjustments in the proportion of macronutrients.
- Maintenance phase: Stabilizes and maintains achievements. Caloric balance and a balanced distribution of macronutrients are sought.
- Recovery phase: Post-competitions or intense periods. Emphasis is placed on nutrients that facilitate the recovery and repair of tissues.

Implementation of Nutritional Periodization

- Identification of objectives: Before beginning, you must identify the objectives of each phase of training. Decide if you are looking to increase muscle mass, improve stamina, reduce fat, or recover from a competition.
- Phase planning: When the objectives have been identified, the phases and their duration are planned. A classic example for bodybuilders would be starting with a bulking phase followed by a cutting phase before a competition.
- Caloric adjustment: Caloric needs will vary according to the phase. In the loading phase, a surplus is sought to support muscle growth, while in the definition phase, a deficit is sought to reduce fat.
- Macronutrients: As well as caloric adjustment, it is crucial to adapt the ratio of macronutrients. For example, during the loading phase, one could consume more carbohydrates to support longer and more intense training sessions.
- Monitoring and adjustments: Nutritional periodization is not a rigid plan. You should monitor progress and make adjustments when necessary.

Benefits of Nutritional Periodization

These are the benefits you will enjoy when implementing this advanced technique for bodybuilders:

- By fueling your body according to the demands of each training phase, you're in a better position to achieve specific adaptations, whether it's hypertrophy, endurance, or recovery.
- You'll gain muscle and lose fat at optimal times, ensuring you're in top shape for competition.
- You lessen your chance of becoming hurt from overtraining or a nutritional deficiency.

Even while it could seem challenging at first, with practice and time you will be able to recognize your body's demands during the various phases and adjust your diet accordingly.

Cheat Days

The term "cheat days" has gained popularity in the world of bodybuilding and dieting. These days provide some people a chance to relax from rigorous dietary restrictions, while others see them as a useful tool that, when utilized properly, enhances performance, body composition, and morale.

A scheduled day off from your normal diet during which you can eat anything you want without feeling restricted in terms of calories, food kinds, or both, is known as a cheat day.

Potential Cheat Day Benefits

During a prolonged diet, especially one that involves a caloric deficit, metabolism decreases as an adaptive mechanism. A temporary increase in calorie intake restarts metabolism and increases thermogenesis.

This day acts as a psychological reinforcement, reducing the feeling of deprivation and helping to maintain motivation; in the same way, it replenishes glycogen stores, which are required for intense training.

How to Implement Cheat Day?

Follow these recommendations:

- Don't let your cheat day be an impulsive decision. Set a date and stick to it, making sure it aligns with your goals.
- While the idea is to allow yourself flexibility, don't view cheat days as an excuse to overeat uncontrollably. Choose foods you enjoy and eat until you feel satisfied, not full.
- Consider scheduling your most intense or energy-demanding workouts the day after your cheat day to take advantage of the glycogen boost.
- Watch how your body responds. If you feel like cheat days work for you, great! If you feel they are hindering your progress, consider adjusting the frequency or focus.

On the other hand, you need to differentiate between a cheat day and a carb reload day. While the former focuses on general dietary flexibility, the latter focuses specifically on increasing carbohydrate intake to improve performance and boost metabolism and is often more controlled.

Professional Adaptation: Incorporating Professional Techniques into Your Routine

The search for the perfect body and optimal performance has led to the development of numerous techniques and strategies by professional bodybuilders. These athletes dedicate their lives to perfecting every detail, from diet to training, and their experience has created a set of practices that benefit anyone, regardless of experience level. Professional adaptation is the act of adopting these advanced methods and customizing them so that you may use them regularly.

First Understand the Body of a Professional

A professional bodybuilder's physique is the product of years of commitment, discipline, and education. Every muscle and fiber bears the marks of long hours of exercise, thoughtful dietary planning, and meticulous rest. Behind the scenes, however, lies a sophisticated system that has undergone extensive adaptation and runs with astounding efficiency. The first step to incorporating expert procedures into your routine is to comprehend this methodology.

The public is drawn to the aesthetics of bodybuilding, yet a biological mechanism that has been well-calibrated lies underneath these stunning displays. Beyond having big, defined muscles, the adaptations are extensive. It entails optimizing the cardiovascular system, effectively using nutrients, and having a steely attitude.

What are the actual advantages of learning about and acquiring a professional's physiology and thinking, then? Optimizing training comes first. You'll be able to customize your workouts to enhance growth and reduce the chance of injury if you have a thorough grasp of how muscles function on a micro and macro level. When you are aware of what a high-performance athlete needs to eat, you may modify your diet to better feed your body and improve recovery and training adaption.

The enhancement of metabolic efficiency is another advantage. A specialist understands precisely when and how to eat to get the best results, and this dietary plan has a big influence on how the body burns calories and gains muscle.

Last but not least, having a comprehensive comprehension of a professional's physique allows you to see the possibilities. It offers you a road map for achieving your objectives and assists you in setting realistic ones. It teaches you to respect the process as much as the outcome and that persistence and devotion are the keys to great success.

How therefore do you go on this road of professional adaptation? Start by being informed. Reading on anatomy, physiology, and sports nutrition should be done. Learn about the most recent advancements in the study of exercise science and bodybuilding.

Then, pay attention to your body, and how it responds as you implement new methods and tactics. Do you feel more powerful? Do you possess greater vigor? How is the healing going? You may enhance your outcomes by learning to decipher these signals and make modifications in real-time.

Periodized Training

This methodology is based on the systematic and scheduled organization of training to improve performance, reduce the risk of injury, and overcome plateaus.

Periodical training first looks to be a succession of training cycles that differ in volume, intensity, and concentration. The purpose of these cycles, or phases, is to get the body ready for the next degree of intensity, allowing for ongoing and gradual adaptations. Beyond this technical definition, periodized training is a potent tool that gives the training process a distinct framework and enables more effective adaptation.

The avoidance of burnout and plateaus is one of the main advantages of regular exercise. Your body won't become accustomed to a certain workout by shifting the emphasis and intensity regularly. This ongoing change prevents muscles from adapting and reaching a plateau, which is when they stop responding. This implies that you will see consistent progress over time with appropriately periodized training.

Another big advantage is the low danger of injury. The same muscle groups or joints are not continually taxed by changing the way you train. This permits recuperation time and lowers the risk of overuse injuries.

Training must address mindset, and periodized training excels in this area. Maintaining strong motivation is achieved by having distinct cycles and objectives. Every cycle's completion represents a minor triumph and a step closer to the ultimate objective.

The use of periodized training is where its true power now lies. Whether you want to build muscle growth, increase your stamina, or get ready for a competition, it's critical to establish a clear goal before you begin. The entire training time is then calculated and divided into cycles, which may last for a few weeks or even a few months.

Every cycle has a distinct focus. For instance, one cycle uses heavier weights and fewer repetitions to emphasize strength. With fewer weights and more reps, the following cycle may concentrate on hypertrophy. The body adjusts as you go through these cycles, getting ready for the next degree of difficulty.

Within this approach, recovery must be taken into account. Including weeks of lower intensity or "de-load weeks" allows the body to recover, reducing the risk of overtraining. These weeks are just as important as the high-intensity weeks and should be an integral part of the plan.

As for nutrition, it must be aligned with the cycle approach. For example, during a strength cycle, you may require more caloric intake, while in a trim cycle, you might reduce caloric intake and focus more on protein and micronutrients.

Rest and Recovery

One of the most underrated aspects of professional training is the importance of rest and recovery. To adapt recovery techniques:

- Take time for active rest: This involves low-intensity activities, such as walking or gentle stretching, that promote recovery without adding stress to the body.
- Consider physical therapy: Massage, salt baths, compression, and other techniques help speed recovery.
- Get enough sleep: Sleep is when your body repairs itself. Make sure you get 7–9 hours of sleep a night.

Incorporating professional techniques into your routine does not mean becoming a professional overnight. It's about taking the best of what professionals do and adapting it to your life, your goals, and your abilities.

Bodybuilding is a personal journey, and each person has a unique path. By learning from the best and adapting their techniques, you accelerate your progress and achieve your goals faster and more effectively. Always remember to listen to your body, continuously educate yourself, and enjoy the process.

Together we have navigated the depths of the secrets that professional bodybuilders hold, uncovering techniques, strategies, and principles that have brought them to the top of their game. These recommendations are the result of years of trial and error, dedication, and perseverance; they are not just theories. The actual value of these suggestions, as I have emphasized throughout this chapter, is in their customized implementation. Everybody's bodies respond differently, and each person has unique objectives, constraints, and capabilities.

With this information at your disposal, I hope you are motivated and equipped to advance your diet and exercise regimen. The route to excellence is never simple, but with the correct resources and attitude, it becomes more comprehensible and feasible.

Remember that real bodybuilding is more than just growing muscles and looking good. It is a commitment to oneself and a celebration of what the body and mind can do when they work in unison.

I want to encourage you to go on with passion and tenacity as I conclude this chapter. You'll have even more tools to improve your technique, diet, and outlook after reading what comes next. Be proud of what you've discovered thus far, but keep in mind that learning never truly ends. Every day offers a fresh chance to develop, discover, and better oneself.

Continue reading as you pursue excellence. You have a world of opportunities before you, and I'll be at your side every step of the way. Let's go!

Chapter 6

Overcoming Food Preparation Obstacles — Practical Solutions

By now, it should be clear that bodybuilding involves more than just lifting weights in the gym. It calls for a commitment to hard work, consistency, good exercise, and—possibly most importantly—an appropriate diet. Meal planning is a crucial tool for athletes on this trip because it enables them to make sure they are consuming the proper nutrients at the appropriate times to improve their performance and recovery.

Meal preparation has its own unique set of difficulties and difficulties, just like any habit or routine. These can include not having enough time or access to the necessary components, as well as losing motivation or being bored with a routine eating schedule. Recognizing and addressing these issues is essential if you want to prevent nutrition from being the weak link in your bodybuilding program.

You must first realize that preparing meals is not a simple process with a single right way to execute it. It is an adaptable procedure that takes into account each person's unique needs, objectives, and circumstances. While some people are able to cook their entire week's budget for meals in a single day, others might need to stretch this out over a few days owing to their hectic schedules. The secret is to discover a method that you can stick with for a very long time and that works for you.

One of the biggest challenges people have when it comes to meal preparation is unquestionably a lack of time. We live in a fast-paced world, where balancing work, training, and social and family life, among other commitments, is overwhelming. Remember that meal preparation is an investment in your health and your bodybuilding goals. It's not about finding time; it's about making time. Often, with a little planning and organization, it is possible to create an efficient system that minimizes time in the kitchen while maximizing the quality and variety of meals.

Another common challenge is access to quality ingredients. Depending on where you live, it would be difficult to find certain foods or supplements for your nutritional plan. In the digital age, numerous alternatives are available. From online stores offering home delivery to local communities promoting sustainable agriculture, solutions are always accessible for those willing to seek them.

Diet stagnation and monotony are other problems many people face. Eating the same foods day after day is boring, while also limiting the variety of nutrients you eat. It is essential to spend time researching new recipes, trying different ingredients, and regularly changing the menu. Variety keeps things interesting and ensures a more complete and balanced nutritional profile.

Cost is an important consideration in meal preparation. While it's true that investing in health through quality nutrition comes at a higher price, there are ways to be strategic and efficient with spending. Buying in bulk, taking advantage of offers and discounts, and choosing local and seasonal foods significantly reduce costs. In the same way, follow the recommendations that I made in Chapter 3.

Last but not least is the challenge of staying motivated. As with any habit, there will be times when meal prep feels like a chore and not an integral part of your bodybuilding journey. At those times, it's crucial to remember the "why" behind your choice to prepare your meals. Whether it's to achieve a personal record, prepare for a competition, or simply improve your overall health, your underlying reason will give you the strength to keep going.

This chapter will be dedicated to addressing each of these obstacles in detail, offering practical solutions and advice based on the experience of bodybuilding professionals and amateurs. At the end of the day, meal preparation is a tool, and like any tool, its effectiveness depends on how it is used. With the right strategies, you will overcome any obstacle and ensure that your nutrition is always aligned with your bodybuilding goals.

Facing Challenges: Navigating Moments of Discontent

Every trip, whether it be personal, professional, or physical, will have its unsatisfactory times. You could even feel like you're going backward at times when you should be getting forward. These times will come, but how you handle them will primarily decide your success and how far you get on your journey.

Understanding Discontent

Before seeking solutions, you must understand the nature of discontent. It does not arise without reason; it is a sign that something is not right or that there are aspects of your life or routine that need adjustments. In the context of bodybuilding, discontent manifests as dissatisfaction with physical progress, exhaustion, injury, or dietary frustrations.

Understanding the source of the problem is necessary before looking for remedies. It doesn't just happen; it is an indication that something is wrong or that you need to make some changes to certain parts of your daily life. Bodybuilders who are dissatisfied with their physical development may feel worn out, injured, or frustrated with their diet.

First and foremost, don't disregard it. Be mindful of your body and thoughts. Where does this emotion originate from, you could ask? Is it a reaction to exhaustion, a poor diet, or unmet expectations?

The Comparison: A Thief of Joy

Comparison is one of the main sources of resentment. Images of perfection are all around us these days, whether they be of athletes showing off their ripped muscles, people lifting heavy objects, or people eating tasty and healthy meals. You begin to doubt your ability to complete the work as a result of this continuous exposure, which leaves you feeling unsatisfied with your progress.

Keep in mind that every person is different, and what you see online just represents a small portion of reality. Similar difficulties to yours are common, although these experiences are rarely discussed. Focus on your path, appreciate your successes, and learn from your failures rather than comparing yourself to others.

Readjustment of Expectations

Unmet expectations can sometimes be the cause of dissatisfaction. While setting high objectives is a fantastic idea, they must also be attainable. Frustration will result if you aim to lose a considerable amount of body fat or put on 20 pounds of muscle in a month.

Think about your objectives again for a moment. Are they feasible given your present situation? Do you allow yourself enough time and funding to do it? Feel free to lower them if you discover that they are too high. It is a sign of maturity and self-awareness rather than weakness.

The Importance of Resilience

Resilience is the ability to bounce back quickly from difficulties and adapt in times of adversity. Cultivating resilience will help you get through moments of discontent without losing sight of your goals.

To build resilience:

- Accept that challenges are part of the process. They are not indicative of failure, but learning opportunities.
- Find a support network. Talking with friends, family, or gym buddies provides a valuable outside perspective on your challenges.
- Celebrate small achievements. Every step forward, however small, is progress.

Recognizing the Need for Rest

Tiredness and fatigue amplify feelings of discontent. If you constantly feel frustrated or dissatisfied with your progress, it could be a sign that you need to rest.

Overtraining is a reality in bodybuilding. Recognize when your body needs a breather. Rest is as important to progress as training and diet. During this time, the body recovers, repairs tissue and muscle, and prepares for future challenges.

Self-Pity: Your Greatest Ally

Being hard on yourself might seem like a way to stay motivated, but in reality, it's counterproductive. Self-compassion involves treating yourself with the same kindness and understanding that you would treat a close friend.

Acknowledge your feelings without judging them. If a workout didn't go your way or you missed a planned meal, instead of beating yourself up, understand that everyone has tough days. What matters is how you choose to move forward.

Adjusting the Strategy

If you're feeling persistent discontent, it might be time to make some adjustments in your approach. Maybe you need to change your training routine, adjust your diet, or consult a trainer or nutritionist.

Don't be afraid to seek outside help. Professionals offer a new perspective and suggest changes you may not have considered. Committing to someone else is a motivational boost to keep going.

Troubleshooting: Your Guide to Food Preparation

The art and science of food preparation is focused on nourishing the body, as well as finding creative and practical solutions to the inevitable challenges that come along the way. Facing these obstacles head-on and with determination will allow you to improve your cooking skills, adapt, and evolve on your bodybuilding journey.

#1: Lack of Time

The modern world bombards us with responsibilities and commitments that often make us feel like there aren't enough hours in the day. Meal prep doesn't have to be a time-consuming task.

Strategies:

- Block prep: Set aside a specific day of the week, like Sunday, to prep most of your meals. Cooking in large quantities allows you to make the most of your time.
- Use efficient tools: Invest in appliances that save you time, such as slow cookers, pressure cookers, or food processors.
- Simple recipes: opt for recipes with fewer ingredients and steps. Sometimes the simplest is the most effective.

#2: Access to Quality Ingredients

Depending on your location and the season, certain foods may not be available or may be too expensive.

Strategies:

- Buy local and in season: Food that is in season is often more affordable and is at its peak of flavor and nutrition.
- Freeze in large quantities: When food is available and at a good price, buy in large quantities and freeze it. That way you'll have a supply during the months when that food isn't in season.
- Specialty stores: International food stores or health stores often carry a wider variety of specific ingredients.

#3: Stagnation and Monotony in the Diet

Repeating the same menu constantly leads to boredom and a lack of motivation.

Strategies:

- Rotate your recipes: If you have a repertoire of 10–15 recipes, rotate between them each week.
- Introduce new ingredients: Experiment with a new ingredient every week.
- Cooking classes: Consider taking a cooking class or workshop to learn new techniques and recipes.

#4: Cost

Maintaining a specialized diet is expensive, this is not a secret, especially if you are focusing on organic foods or high-quality supplements.

Strategies:

- Plan your meals: By having a clear plan, you avoid buying unnecessary food that ends up being wasted.
- Buy in bulk: Buying food in bulk is often cheaper in the long run.
- Grow your food: Even a small garden or a few pots will give you fresh herbs and some vegetables.

#5: Loss of Motivation

As with any habit, there will be times when meal prep feels more like an obligation than an integral part of your bodybuilding routine.

Strategies:

- Set clear goals: Remembering why you started preparing your meals gives you the momentum you need to continue.
- Join a group: Whether online or in person, joining a community of like-minded people is inspiring.
- Document your progress: Keep a food journal and see how it correlates with your energy levels, gym performance, and other health indicators.

#6: Nutritional Complexity

With so much information available it is difficult to decipher the best nutritional approach for your specific needs.

Strategies:

- Consult a professional: A nutritionist or dietitian will give you a personalized guide adapted to your goals and needs.
- Continuing education: Spend time reading books, articles, and studies on nutrition. Always check the sources and make sure the information comes from experts in the field.
- Trial and error: Sometimes it takes a little experimentation to determine what works best for your body. Write down how you feel with different nutritional approaches and adjust as needed.

At the end of the day, meal prep is a combination of science and art, it will require adaptability and perseverance. Proactively facing challenges and looking for effective solutions allows you to ensure that your nutrition is a driving force on your path to bodybuilding success. With the right guidance and strategies, any obstacle becomes an opportunity to learn, adapt, and grow.

Making Meal Prep a Habit: The Importance of Regularity

While determination and stamina are necessary to withstand the rigors of training, meal preparation ensures that all those efforts are not wasted. Done properly, it turns out to be a boon, giving bodybuilders the correct nutritional intake needed to fuel their bodies and recover properly. When viewed from the perspective of its long-term benefits, and its importance is understood, homework begins to take on new meaning, becoming an act of self-care. It is an investment of time that is made once a week, or even daily, to ensure that you have a constant supply of healthy and adequate food to meet nutritional demands.

It is important to note that this is not a static task. Adaptability and flexibility are needed since not every week is the same. Sometimes unexpected challenges get in the way, but with proper planning and an open mind, you will overcome these challenges. The key is in anticipation and organization.

Understanding the psychology behind habit formation will allow you to move faster toward your goals. Humans are creatures of habit, and repetition is the surest path to lasting habit formation. This is particularly true in the case of meal preparation. By coming to understand the cycle of trigger, routine, and reward, you can establish a structure that makes regular meal preparation easier.

One might ask, why is regularity in meal preparation so crucial? Well, the answer is simple. Consistency in the diet is one of the main determinants of success in bodybuilding. While proper workouts are vital, nutrition provides the tools necessary to build and repair muscle.

The process begins long before the stove is turned on or a pan is pulled out. It starts with research and knowledge. Knowing which foods are best for your body type and specific bodybuilding goals is critical. Once you have that knowledge, proceed to planning.

Planning is a crucial stage. It's not just about deciding which meals to prepare, you must determine the portions, calculate the macros, and make sure that all the nutrients are present. This seems like a lot of work at first, but over time, it becomes second nature. As you become more versed in the art of food preparation, you discover tricks and techniques that simplify the process.

Of course, execution is important. This is where dedication comes into play. Spending a few hours a week cooking and preparing your meals is a big investment of time, but the benefits far outweigh the initial effort. Imagine not having to worry about what to eat after a grueling workout or not having to succumb to fast food temptations because you don't have a healthy meal on hand.

The act of preparing meals regularly has psychological benefits. It brings a sense of control over your diet, which is hugely empowering. When you know exactly what you are consuming, the uncertainty factor is removed.

Regular meal preparation instills discipline, an indispensable quality for any serious bodybuilder. It requires planning, effort, and dedication, just like training sessions. It could be argued that meal preparation and training go hand in hand, each complementing and reinforcing the other.

Bravo! You've reached the end of Chapter 6, and with that, you've navigated through some of the most common challenges and practical solutions in the world of bodybuilding meal prep. You should be proud of yourself for the commitment and determination you have shown in immersing yourself in this reading. It's no small task to tackle these challenges, and every page you've read demonstrates your dedication to perfecting your art and taking the best care of your body.

But the journey does not end here. As you progress through the book, you'll come across even more insights and strategies designed to take you to the next level. So, I encourage you to keep going. You are on a path of growth and transformation, and each chapter you read brings you one step closer to your best version. Go ahead and keep conquering your goals!

Chapter 7
From Fitness Enthusiast to Professional Athlete – Your Way Forward

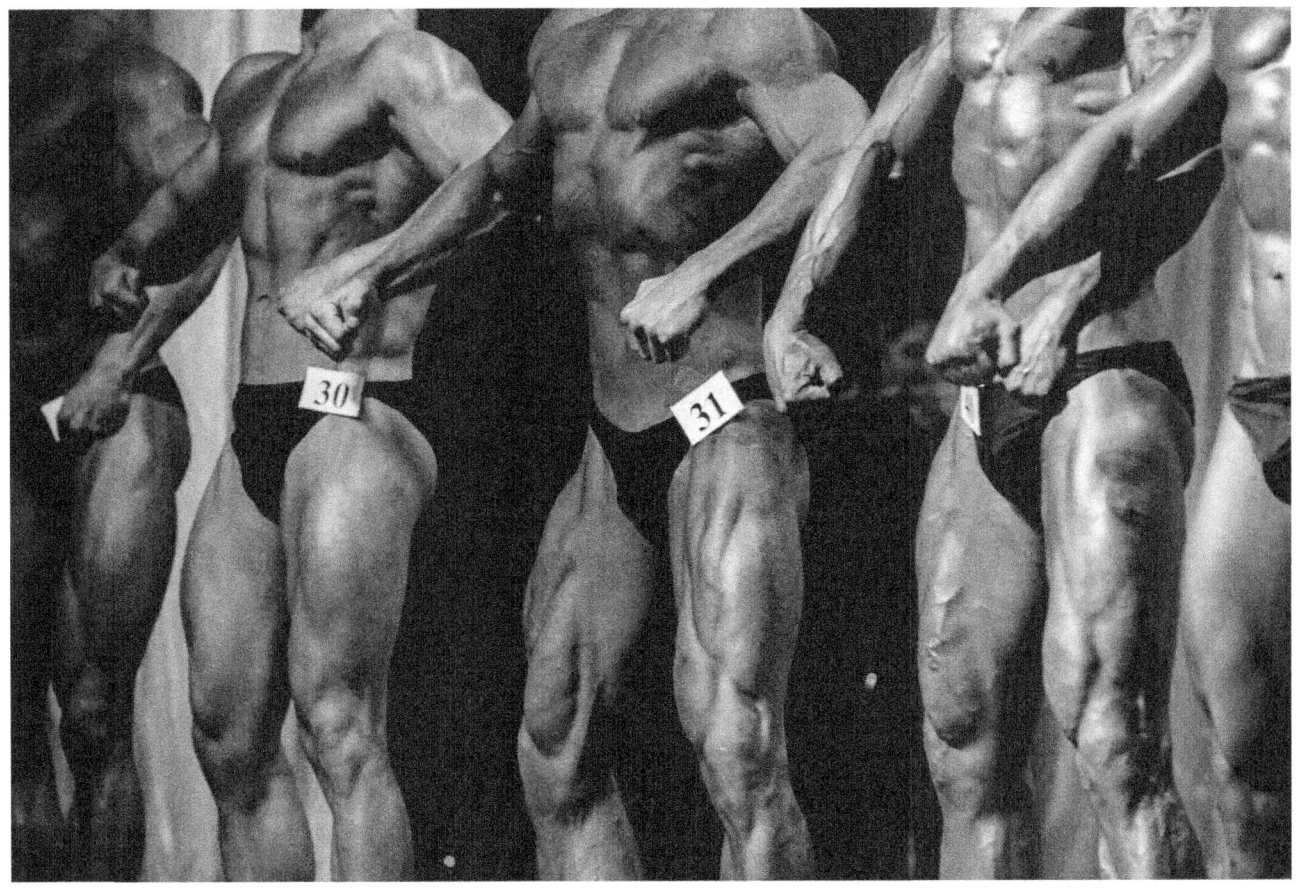

Many people start as simple fitness enthusiasts, watching great athletes from afar, drawing inspiration from their exploits, and harboring dreams of reaching that level of excellence one day. While that initial fervor is required to ignite the spark, going from amateur to professional athlete requires much more than passion. It requires dedication, learning, adaptation, and, most importantly, a clear vision of the destination.

The attitude, in addition to the physical element, is crucial to this development. A resilient attitude enables professional athletes to overcome challenges, adjust to shifting conditions, and endure.

Because each individual is different, what functions for one person may not function for another. However, some principles and lessons are universal. While becoming a bodybuilding professional is challenging, it is incredibly rewarding. Every sacrifice and every challenge are steps toward excellence. In the end, it's about a commitment to excellence and a burning desire to be the best version of yourself.

Raise Your Game: Advancing Your Bodybuilding Journey

Bodybuilding is a combination of art and science as well as a test of tenacity and patience. Beyond having a great body, the prize is the profound self-knowledge and mental fortitude gained during the exercise. However, how do you advance your bodybuilding enthusiasm and get professional status? Here are some crucial suggestions to continue on your journey:

Find a Mentor

Having a mentor who has traveled the journey before and is willing to guide you is one of the most important advantages of bodybuilding. You may acquire experience, information, and networks through the correct mentoring, which will hasten your advancement. Instead of merely looking for someone with muscles, choose someone with experience in the activity.

Continuing Education

The bodybuilding industry is enormous and ever-changing. Spend time educating yourself, training techniques, nutrition, recovery, sports psychology, and more. Become a perpetual student of the game.

Develop Your Mindset

Mental stamina is just as crucial as physical strength. Learn to manage frustration, fatigue, and fear. Use visualization and meditation techniques to keep a positive and focused mindset, even when the going gets tough.

Set Clear Goals

Knowing exactly what you want to achieve helps you draw up a more effective plan. Whether it's increasing your muscle mass, improving your definition, or preparing for a specific competition, have a clear goal in mind and review it regularly.

Compete

Nothing tests you like competing. It confronts you with your fears, challenges you to be your best, and provides valuable feedback on where you are on your journey. Even if you don't aspire to be a professional, competing gives you a new perspective on your training and skills.

Learn From Your Failures

Not everything will be a bed of roses. There will be times when you feel like you are not progressing or even regressing. Instead of getting discouraged, analyze these moments. Find the hidden lessons and use them as a springboard to your next achievements.

Prioritize Recovery

As you intensify your workouts, recovery becomes even more necessary. Invest in sports massages, mobility therapies, and relaxation techniques. Take time to stretch and consider incorporating practices like yoga to improve flexibility and balance.

Build a Community

Surrounding yourself with people with similar goals keeps you motivated and provides you with a support network on tough days. Whether it's at your local gym, bodybuilding club, or online groups, seek out those who share your passion and commitment.

Innovate and Adapt

What worked for you in the early stages of your journey may not be as effective as you go on. Don't be afraid to change your routines, try new supplements, or experiment with different techniques. Adaptability is a sign of an evolved athlete.

Professionalize Your Approach

If you truly aspire to become a professional athlete, treat your training and nutrition with the seriousness they deserve. This could mean investing in high-quality equipment, pursuing advanced training programs, or even considering bodybuilding as a possible career.

The bodybuilding journey is deep and personal. As you seek to progress from enthusiast to professional, remember that the journey itself is just as significant as the destination. Every lift, every meal, and every night of rest are pieces of the puzzle that lead you toward the strongest, most disciplined version of yourself. Enjoy the process, constantly learn and, above all, believe in yourself. The world of professional bodybuilding awaits you.

Ready, Set, Go: Preparing for Competitions and Races

When you decide to take the bold step and take on a bodybuilding competition or race, you are not only committing yourself to showing off your physique, but to a total transformation that encompasses mind, body, and spirit. Competing takes your dedication to bodybuilding to a new level and requires impeccable focus and discipline. Here, I'll walk you through the process of getting ready so you may walk on stage with confidence and in top form.

Identifying your motives is the first and most crucial step. What motivates you to compete? Knowing why you're doing something, whether it's for personal fulfillment, to push your boundaries, or in the hopes of earning professional acclaim, will give you the drive you need on the hardest days. Your compass will be this clarity, especially in trying times.

Once you've made up your mind, it's time to come up with a plan. Depending on your starting point, a full competition preparation takes anywhere from a few months to a year or more. If you're considering a bodybuilding competition, you'll need to work on specifics: cut and definition, volume, posing, and presentation. Each of these elements requires attention and time.

If this is your first time, you could opt for a local or regional competition to gain experience. Study the rules and categories of the competition to ensure that your preparation is in line with what is expected.

Nutritionally, it is crucial to adjust your diet as you get closer to the date of the competition. You'll increase your protein intake and moderate carbohydrates, all while maintaining a proper balance of micronutrients to ensure your body is functioning optimally. You may need to reduce your caloric intake to achieve extreme definition, but you must do it in a controlled and healthy way. Dehydration is a strategy in the days leading up to the event, but remember, always prioritize your health.

The training will intensify. In addition to your regular weight-lifting routines, you'll likely incorporate more cardio to aid fat loss. Be careful not to overdo it and fall into overtraining. Listen to your body and give it the rest it needs.

Practicing your posing is essential. It is not enough to have an impressive physique; you should know how to present it. Consider working with a posing coach who can guide you in the best ways to highlight your strengths and minimize your weaknesses.

Emotionally and mentally, you will face challenges. There will be days of doubt, where you will question your ability or if all the effort is worth it. At such times, remember your initial motivations. Visualize the moment you stand on that stage, under the lights, showing the world your dedication and passion.

Finally, presentation is key. Choose the right competition clothing that fits well and highlights your best features. Consider other elements, such as tanning and makeup, that further enhance your stage performance.

Preparing for a bodybuilding competition or race is one of the most rewarding and challenging experiences you can undertake. It requires total dedication, but the benefits, learning, and satisfaction you get are unmatched. When you finally find yourself behind the curtain, ready to go on stage, take a deep breath, trust your preparation, and enjoy the moment. It's your time to shine.

The previous chapters were conceived to prepare you to evolve as a bodybuilder and athlete until you reach a professional level, so follow and practice all the recommendations.

Fuel for Motivation: Fanning the Flames of Determination

The world of bodybuilding is unique and full of specific challenges and rewards that require a special type of motivation. Those who aspire to enter competitions need more than well-defined muscles; they need fiery determination. These are some key points that fuel that motivation:

Clear Vision of the Desired Physique

In bodybuilding, the power of visualization is immense. Having a clear picture of what you want your body to look like not only guides your training but also fuels the passion to work toward that goal.

Establish Short-Term Micro-Goals

At a professional level, the road to victory can seem long and sometimes overwhelming. Break that path down into more manageable, short-term micro-goals. It can be as detailed as improving 1% in certain aspects each week. By achieving these small goals, not only will you see steady progress, but each achievement will act as positive reinforcement, rekindling your motivation and giving you confidence in your ability to conquer the ultimate goal.

Inspirational Stories

Learn the stories of the greats of bodybuilding. The careers of legends like Arnold Schwarzenegger or Ronnie Coleman can be the spark that ignites your internal fire. Understanding their struggles and successes reminds you that, with determination, anything is possible.

Competence as a Measurer

Taking part in small competitions, even before you feel completely ready, can offer invaluable perspective. These experiences give you a clear idea of where you are and what areas you need to improve, and nothing motivates you more than wanting to push your own limits.

Recognition of Progress

In bodybuilding, physical changes do not happen overnight. It is essential to keep track of your progress, whether through photographs, measurements, or notes on your performance. Seeing how you have moved forward, no matter how small the change, is a powerful motivator.

Rituals and Routines

Establish pre- and post-workout rituals that help you mentally connect with your goals. Whether it's an uplifting song, a stretching routine, or even visualizing your goals before training, these rituals will keep you focused and on track.

Meditation and Guided Visualization

Many elite athletes have spoken about the effectiveness of visualization in their preparation. Spend time each week in guided meditation and imagery, imagining yourself in competition, pushing your limits, and ultimately achieving victory. Feel the excitement, the adrenaline, and the pride. This mental practice will emotionally connect you to your goals and act as a powerful reminder of what you are pursuing, fanning those flames of determination.

Bodybuilding is as much a mental journey as it is a physical one. Constantly feed your motivation with these tools and you will see how, with determination and effort, you will get closer and closer to the top of the competition.

Bonus:
30-Day Customizable Meal Plan

Congratulations! You have reached the end of this transformative journey and you are on the threshold of the last chapter, a very special bonus designed exclusively for you. By putting time, effort, and passion into every page, you've gained invaluable insights, advanced techniques, and pro tips to raise your game in the world of bodybuilding. Now, to finish with a flourish, I present to you a gift that will consolidate all the nutritional principles discussed: a customizable 30-day meal plan.

This plan is not simply a dietary guide; is a powerful tool designed to boost your energy, optimize your recovery, and maximize your results. You already know that nutrition is the cornerstone of any training regimen, and this plan has been meticulously crafted to respond to the specific needs of those committed to bodybuilding.

What makes this bond unique is its ability to adapt. Although it gives you a clear structure and direction, it is designed to customize it according to your requirements, tastes, and objectives. This is your plan, a road map that will accompany you in the coming weeks and will help you to physically manifest all the effort and dedication that you have invested in this path.

Celebrate this moment, because you are about to access a tool that will be the perfect complement to your training and commitment. It is time to merge theory and practice, to bring everything you have learned to the plate, and to enjoy the fruits of your labor. Welcome to the book's special bonus, your customizable 30-day meal plan!

Customize Your Approach: Customizing Your Plan

The following plan is strictly based on the recipes presented in Chapter 4. You will find that some recipes are repeated, which is unavoidable due to the number of recipes, but you will notice that they are still distributed in a very convenient way.

I have not included the preparation of the recipes, because you will simply have to look at the day and the title of the recipe and go to Chapter 4 to know the ingredients, nutritional table, cooking time, and preparation:

Day 1:

- **Breakfast:** Spinach and Feta Cheese Omelet
- **Mid-morning snack:** Turkey and Cheese Wraps
- **Lunch:** Grilled Chicken With Quinoa and Broccoli
- **Mid-afternoon snack:** Tuna and Avocado Rolls
- **Dinner:** Grilled Turkey With Roasted Vegetables
- **Pre-workout:** Egg White Pancakes
- **Post-workout:** Banana Protein Shake

Day 2:

- **Breakfast:** Oatmeal and Banana Energy Smoothie
- **Mid-morning snack:** Strawberry and Almond Protein Smoothie
- **Lunch:** Baked Salmon With Chickpea Salad
- **Mid-afternoon snack:** Chickpea and Red Pepper Dip
- **Dinner:** Sautéed Tofu With Sesame and Vegetables
- **Pre-workout:** Chickpea and Tuna Salad
- **Post-workout:** Chicken Breast With Quinoa and Vegetables

Day 3:

- **Breakfast:** Breakfast Burrito With Egg and Black Beans
- **Mid-morning snack:** Protein Granola Bars
- **Lunch:** Asian-Style Beef With Broccoli
- **Mid-afternoon snack:** Curry Chicken Bites
- **Dinner:** Tuna Salad With Avocado and Tomato

- **Pre-workout:** Quinoa With Vegetables and Chicken
- **Post-workout:** Quinoa With Chicken and Broccoli

Day 4:

- **Breakfast:** Fruit Smoothie With Protein
- **Mid-morning snack:** Tofu and Pepper Skewers
- **Lunch:** Lentils With Spinach and Hard-Boiled Egg
- **Mid-afternoon snack:** Stuffed Eggs With Chicken
- **Dinner:** Teriyaki Chicken With Broccoli
- **Pre-workout:** Tuna and Avocado Wrap
- **Post-workout:** Tuna and Chickpea Salad

Day 5:

- **Breakfast:** Baked Eggs With Asparagus and Tomatoes
- **Mid-morning snack:** Egg Rolls With Vegetables and Chicken
- **Lunch:** Turkey Meatballs
- **Mid-afternoon snack:** Mini Portobello Pizzas With Ricotta Cheese
- **Dinner:** Zucchini Spaghetti With Turkey Meatballs
- **Pre-workout:** Rice and Egg Bowl With Spinach
- **Post-workout:** Rice With Chicken and Vegetables

Day 6:

- **Breakfast:** Egg and Turkey Rolls
- **Mid-morning snack:** Turkey and Cheese Wraps
- **Lunch:** Whole Wheat Pasta With Tuna and Arugula
- **Mid-afternoon snack:** Chickpea and Red Pepper Dip
- **Dinner:** Grilled Salmon With Asparagus
- **Pre-workout:** Quinoa With Vegetables and Tofu
- **Post-workout:** Turkey and Quinoa Salad

Day 7:

- **Breakfast:** Yogurt and Granola Parfait
- **Mid-morning snack:** Tuna and Avocado Rolls
- **Lunch:** Grilled Chicken With Quinoa and Vegetables
- **Mid-afternoon snack:** Wrapped Tuna in Lettuce
- **Dinner:** Chicken Fajitas
- **Pre-workout:** Rice and Egg Bowl With Spinach
- **Post-workout:** Whole Grain Pasta With Chicken and Broccoli

Day 8:

- **Breakfast:** Chia and Red Fruit Parfait
- **Mid-morning snack:** Turkey Skewers With Yogurt Sauce
- **Lunch:** Baked Salmon With Brussels Sprouts and Almonds
- **Mid-afternoon snack:** Chicken and Black Bean Quesadillas
- **Dinner:** Beef Steak With Mushrooms
- **Pre-workout:** Chicken Breast With Almond Sauce
- **Post-workout:** Whole Grain Pasta With Tuna

Day 9:

- **Breakfast:** Chickpea Waffles
- **Mid-morning snack:** Turkey and Cheese Wraps
- **Lunch:** Chickpea Salad With Chicken and Avocado
- **Mid-afternoon snack:** Protein Granola Bars
- **Dinner:** Garlic Shrimp With Broccoli
- **Pre-workout:** Lentil and Chorizo Soup
- **Post-workout:** Brown Rice With Shrimp and Peas

Day 10:

- **Breakfast:** Cottage and Fruit Bowl
- **Mid-morning snack:** Chickpea and Red Pepper Dip
- **Lunch:** Turkey in Honey Mustard Sauce
- **Mid-afternoon snack:** Curry Chicken Bites
- **Dinner:** Teriyaki Tofu With Brown Rice
- **Pre-workout:** Chocolate and Peanut Butter Smoothie
- **Post-workout:** Turkey Rolls With Hummus and Peppers

Day 11:

- **Breakfast:** Breakfast Burrito With Egg and Black Beans
- **Mid-morning snack:** Turkey and Cheese Wraps
- **Lunch:** Grilled Tuna With Quinoa Salad
- **Mid-afternoon snack:** Chickpea and Red Pepper Dip
- **Dinner:** Turkey Meatballs With Tomato Sauce
- **Pre-workout:** Egg White Pancakes
- **Post-workout:** Lentil and Tuna Salad

Day 12:

- **Breakfast:** Fruit Smoothie With Protein

- **Mid-morning snack:** Chicken and Black Bean Quesadillas
- **Lunch:** Grilled Chicken With Sweet Potatoes and Asparagus
- **Mid-afternoon snack:** Green Protein Smoothie
- **Dinner:** Tuna Salad With Avocado and Tomato
- **Pre-workout:** Quinoa With Vegetables and Chicken
- **Post-workout:** Tuna Salad With Chickpeas

Day 13:

- **Breakfast:** Chia and Red Fruit Parfait
- **Mid-morning snack:** Egg Rolls With Vegetables and Chicken
- **Lunch:** Grilled Chicken With Sweet Potatoes and Asparagus
- **Mid-afternoon snack:** Protein Granola Bars
- **Dinner:** Grilled Turkey With Roasted Vegetables
- **Pre-workout:** Tuna and Avocado Wrap
- **Post-workout:** Banana Protein Shake

Day 14:

- **Breakfast:** Chickpea Waffles
- **Mid-morning snack:** Curry Chicken Bites
- **Lunch:** Lentils With Spinach and Hard-Boiled Egg
- **Mid-afternoon snack:** Strawberry and Almond Protein Smoothie
- **Dinner:** Beef Steak With Mushrooms
- **Pre-workout:** Quinoa With Vegetables and Tofu
- **Post-workout:** Turkey and Quinoa Salad

Day 15:

- **Breakfast:** Baked Eggs With Asparagus and Tomatoes
- **Mid-morning snack:** Tofu and Pepper Skewers
- **Lunch:** Turkey Meatballs
- **Mid-afternoon snack:** Tuna and Avocado Rolls
- **Dinner:** Tuna Salad With Avocado and Tomato
- **Pre-workout:** Rice and Egg Bowl With Spinach
- **Post-workout:** Whole Grain Pasta With Chicken and Broccoli

Day 16:

- **Breakfast:** Cottage Bowl With Fruit and Almonds
- **Mid-morning snack:** Mini Portobello Pizzas With Ricotta Cheese
- **Lunch:** Baked Salmon With Chickpea Salad
- **Mid-afternoon snack:** Stuffed Eggs With Chicken

- **Dinner:** Sautéed Tofu With Sesame and Vegetables
- **Pre-workout:** Egg White Pancakes
- **Post-workout:** Quinoa With Chicken and Broccoli

Day 17:

- **Breakfast:** Spinach and Feta Cheese Omelet
- **Mid-morning snack:** Chickpea and Red Pepper Dip
- **Lunch:** Asian-Style Beef With Broccoli
- **Mid-afternoon snack:** Protein Granola Bars
- **Dinner:** Grilled Salmon With Asparagus
- **Pre-workout:** Quinoa With Vegetables and Chicken
- **Post-workout:** Tuna Salad With Chickpeas

Day 18:

- **Breakfast:** Chicken and Avocado Wrap
- **Mid-morning snack:** Egg Rolls With Vegetables and Chicken
- **Lunch:** Whole Wheat Pasta With Tuna and Arugula
- **Mid-afternoon snack:** Wrapped Tuna in Lettuce
- **Dinner:** Chicken Fajitas
- **Pre-workout:** Rice and Egg Bowl With Spinach
- **Post-workout:** Brown Rice With Shrimp and Peas

Day 19:

- **Breakfast:** Egg and Turkey Rolls
- **Mid-morning snack:** Strawberry and Almond Protein Smoothie
- **Lunch:** Baked Salmon With Brussels Sprouts and Almonds
- **Mid-afternoon snack:** Curry Chicken Bites
- **Dinner:** Teriyaki Chicken With Broccoli
- **Pre-workout:** Quinoa With Vegetables and Tofu
- **Post-workout:** Whole Grain Pasta With Tuna

Day 20:

- **Breakfast:** Yogurt and Granola Parfait
- **Mid-morning snack:** Turkey and Cheese Wraps
- **Lunch:** Turkey in Honey Mustard Sauce
- **Mid-afternoon snack:** Tuna and Avocado Rolls
- **Dinner:** Zucchini Spaghetti With Turkey Meatballs
- **Pre-workout:** Tuna and Avocado Wrap
- **Post-workout:** Lentil and Tuna Salad

Day 21:

- **Breakfast:** Breakfast Burrito With Egg and Black Beans
- **Mid-morning snack:** Strawberry and Almond Protein Smoothie
- **Lunch:** Grilled Tuna With Quinoa Salad
- **Mid-afternoon snack:** Chicken and Black Bean Quesadillas
- **Dinner:** Teriyaki Tofu With Brown Rice

Day 22:

- **Breakfast:** Fruit Smoothie With Protein
- **Mid-morning snack:** Tuna and Avocado Rolls
- **Lunch:** Chickpea Salad With Chicken and Avocado
- **Mid-afternoon snack:** Protein Granola Bars
- **Dinner:** Garlic Shrimp With Broccoli
- **Pre-workout:** Quinoa With Vegetables and Chicken
- **Post-workout:** Whole Grain Pasta With Tuna

Day 23:

- **Breakfast:** Yogurt and Granola Parfait
- **Mid-morning snack:** Green Protein Smoothie
- **Lunch:** Grilled Chicken With Sweet Potatoes and Asparagus
- **Mid-afternoon snack:** Egg Rolls With Vegetables and Chicken
- **Dinner:** Turkey Meatballs With Tomato Sauce
- **Pre-workout:** Rice and Egg Bowl With Spinach
- **Post-workout:** Brown Rice With Shrimp and Peas

Day 24:

- **Breakfast:** Chickpea Waffles
- **Mid-morning snack:** Curry Chicken Bites
- **Lunch:** Grilled Chicken With Quinoa and Broccoli
- **Mid-afternoon snack:** Chickpea and Red Pepper Dip
- **Dinner:** Tuna Salad With Avocado and Tomato

Day 25:

- **Breakfast:** Cottage and Fruit Bowl
- **Mid-morning snack:** Strawberry and Almond Protein Smoothie
- **Lunch:** Baked Salmon With Mediterranean Chickpea Salad
- **Mid-afternoon snack:** Mini Portobello Pizzas With Ricotta Cheese
- **Dinner:** Grilled Salmon With Asparagus

- **Pre-workout:** Quinoa With Vegetables and Tofu
- **Post-workout:** Tuna Salad With Chickpeas

Day 26:

- **Breakfast:** Baked Eggs With Asparagus and Tomatoes
- **Mid-morning snack:** Tuna and Avocado Rolls
- **Lunch:** Asian-Style Beef With Broccoli
- **Mid-afternoon snack:** Chicken and Black Bean Quesadillas
- **Dinner:** Grilled Turkey With Roasted Vegetables
- **Pre-workout:** Tuna and Avocado Wrap
- **Post-workout:** Quinoa With Chicken and Broccoli

Day 27:

- **Breakfast:** Spinach and Feta Cheese Omelet
- **Mid-morning snack:** Tofu and Pepper Skewers
- **Lunch:** Turkey Meatballs
- **Mid-afternoon snack:** Chickpea and Red Pepper Dip
- **Dinner:** Beef Steak With Mushrooms
- **Pre-workout:** Chickpea and Tuna Salad
- **Post-workout:** Chicken Breast With Quinoa and Vegetables

Day 28:

- **Breakfast:** Oatmeal and Banana Energy Smoothie
- **Mid-morning snack:** Stuffed Eggs With Chicken
- **Lunch:** Whole Wheat Pasta With Tuna and Arugula
- **Mid-afternoon snack:** Turkey Skewers With Yogurt Sauce
- **Dinner:** Zucchini Spaghetti With Turkey Meatballs

Day 29:

- **Breakfast:** Egg and Turkey Rolls
- **Mid-morning snack:** Turkey and Cheese Wraps
- **Lunch:** Baked Salmon With Brussels Sprouts and Almonds
- **Mid-afternoon snack:** Egg Rolls With Vegetables and Chicken
- **Dinner:** Chicken Fajitas
- **Pre-workout:** Rice and Egg Bowl With Spinach
- **Post-workout:** Fruit Smoothie With Protein

Day 30:

- **Breakfast:** Chia and Red Fruit Parfait

- **Mid-morning snack:** Mini Portobello Pizzas With Ricotta Cheese
- **Lunch:** Grilled Chicken With Quinoa and Broccoli
- **Mid-afternoon snack:** Protein Granola Bars
- **Dinner:** Sautéed Tofu With Sesame and Vegetables
- **Pre-workout:** Egg White Pancakes
- **Post-workout:** Whole Grain Pasta With Tuna

Conclusion
Achieving Success Through Effective Meal Planning

The journey has been extensive, informative, and transformative. By reaching these last pages, you have demonstrated your interest in the world of bodybuilding and nutrition, and your commitment and determination to reach a higher version of yourself. Throughout each chapter, the secrets elite athletes have used to sculpt their bodies and achieve their goals have been uncovered, and now it's your turn to apply this knowledge on your path to excellence.

The essence of this book lies in its holistic approach. It was not just about eating well or following a specific routine, but about understanding the deep relationship between the body and the mind. Through meal planning and preparation you fuel your physique, nourish your mind, and gain the clarity and focus to keep going, even when the challenges seem insurmountable.

Bodybuilding is both an art and a science. It is a journey of self-discovery, discipline, and passion. Every lift, every rep, and every meal are conscious decisions to get you closer to your goals. A carefully thought-out and individualized diet enhances performance, speeds up recuperation, and fortifies the mind and soul, giving you the fortitude to face challenges head-on.

You have to realize that your devotion is what will actually bring about change. It's essential to exercise discipline, consistency, and an openness to learning and adapting. Because everybody is different, what works for one person may not work for another. So, I urge you to apply what you've learned and adjust it to fit your requirements and goals.

Let's not forget the importance of adaptability. As I mentioned to you in earlier chapters, changing from a fitness enthusiast to a professional athlete needs a mental shift. To compete at the top, one must have an extreme degree of commitment, concentration, and endurance. The road to success is in your grasp if you have the necessary resources and a persistent mentality.

Keep in mind that while preparing meals is a necessary step on this path, happiness, and general well-being also matter. Maintaining a positive and fruitful relationship with bodybuilding requires striking a balance between effort and self-care, commitment, and downtime.

Last but not least, I want you to pause and consider how far you've come. You have learned a ton from the first page lot the last, giving you a leg up in your quest to become a bodybuilder. You have resources, advice, and methods at your disposal to help you move closer to your objectives.

The conclusion of this book doesn't signal the end of your trip; rather, it ushers in a brand-new one. You are now in the fortunate position of being able to put everything you've learned into practice and see the results of your effort in every muscle, every drop of perspiration, and every dietary decision.

I wish you newfound self-assurance and enthusiasm for bodybuilding. May you persevere through every obstacle, rejoice in every success, no matter how tiny, and never lose sight of your vision or objectives.

I appreciate you joining me on this adventure. It's now your chance to progress, conquer, and attain greatness since the horizon is clear and the way is mapped out. There are no boundaries to what you can do if you work hard, are passionate about what you do, and plan your meals well. Let your career in the world of bodybuilding begin with this, if you like!

List of Ingredients in Alphabetical Order

A

Almond butter

Almond milk

Almonds

Arugula

Asparagus

Avocado

B

Balsamic vinegar

Bamboo shoots

Banana

Basil

Beef steak

Berries

Black olives

Black pepper

Blackberries

Broccoli

Brussels sprouts

C

Canned tuna

Carrots

Celery

Cherry tomatoes

Chia seeds

Chicken

Chicken breast

Chickpea flour

Chives

Cinnamon

Cocoa powder

Cooked black beans

Cooked chickpeas

Cottage cheese

Cucumber

Curry powder

D

Dehydrated cranberries

Dijon mustard

Dried dill

E

Egg whites

Eggs

F

Feta cheese

Fresh ginger

Fresh parsley

Fresh rosemary

Fresh spinach

Fresh tuna loin

Frozen fruits

Fruit mix

G

Garlic

Garlic powder

Granola

Grated cheddar cheese

Grated Parmesan cheese

Greek yogurt

Green onion

Green pepper

H

Honey

Hummus

I

Integral rice

K

Ketchup

Kiwi

l

Lemon

Lemon juice

Lentils

Lettuce

Low-fat cheese

Low-fat mayonnaise

M

Marinara sauce

Milk

Minced turkey meat

Mushrooms

Mustard

O

Oatmeal

Olive oil

Onion

Oregano

P

Peanut butter

Peas

Portobello Mushrooms

Protein powder

Purple Onion

R

Red pepper
Ricotta cheese
Romaine lettuce

S

Salmon
Salmon fillets
Salt
Sausage
Sesame
Sesame oil
Sesame seeds
Shrimp
Smoked salmon
Soy sauce
Spinach
Strawberries

T

Tahini sauce
Teriyaki sauce
Tofu
Tomato
Turkey
Turkey breast

V

Veal (lean fillet)

W

Walnuts
Water
Whole wheat tortillas
Wholemeal bread

Y

Yams
Yogurt

Exclusive bonus

Dear Reader,

First and foremost, I want to extend my heartfelt gratitude to you for choosing and investing your time in my book, "Bodybuilding Meal Prep." Your support means the world to me, and I sincerely hope that the recipes and insights shared within these pages have inspired and empowered you on your bodybuilding journey.

As you've reached the final pages, it's clear that you've dedicated yourself to exploring and embracing the world of nutritious and delicious bodybuilding meals. I am truly honored to have been a part of your journey, and I would be incredibly grateful to hear about your experience.

If this book has added value to your fitness routine and culinary adventures, I kindly invite you to share your thoughts and feedback by leaving a review on Amazon. Your honest review not only helps me to continually improve and provide valuable content, but it also assists fellow fitness enthusiasts in finding a resource that can aid them in their own journey.

As a token of my appreciation for your support and to add even more value to your bodybuilding endeavors, I have prepared a special bonus document just for you! This exclusive content is designed to complement the recipes and tips provided in the book, giving you additional tools and insights to enhance your meal prep and fitness routine.

Accessing your bonus is easy! Simply scan the QR code below, and you'll be directed to download the document instantly. It's my way of saying thank you and ensuring that you have all the resources you need to succeed.

From the depths of my heart, I extend my deepest gratitude for accompanying me on this journey. Your unwavering support and dedication fuel my passion to persistently create and disseminate meaningful content within the realm of Bodybuilding.

Best regards,

Mark J. Lewis

Printed in Great Britain
by Amazon

38169948R00104